Endorsements for carried.

"Justin and Jeremy have done an excellent job in motivating the church to express the love and grace of Jesus our Lord in a world that is desperate for it. I recommend that you read *carried.* to be inspired. It is a good devotional read but, be careful; it will challenge you to be more than just a church attendee. You just might hear God saying, "Come, follow Me.""
—**Pastor Gary Buchman**, Taneytown Baptist Church.

"Just finished reading *carried.* It is an amazing book about an amazing God doing amazing things through pretty normal people. Thanks to Justin and Jeremy (who I haven't had the opportunity to meet yet) for letting God use you guys."
—**Jamie Caldwell**, Student pastor at Northwest Baptist Church.

"It is easy to become accustomed to the feeling of comfort in today's world, and easy to forget about the poor and sick around us. *carried.* is a book that will set your heart on fire for God and encourage you to act on your passions to help people in need around the globe. It will inspire you, challenge you, and change you; it has done just that for me, so I recommend it to all."
—**Kali Fairchild**, Operation.Net.

"After reading *carried.* you will be faced with a decision to make: you can A) put the book down, pat the guys on the back and say "very inspirational, thank you Justin and Jeremy, I have warm fuzzies all over". Or B) you can accept the reality that your heart has been exposed and there is something in your life that must change. You must join the mission of Jesus in bringing the good news to the afflicted and binding up the broken hearted. I am convinced God beckons us to do the latter."
—**Pete Green**, Youth pastor with Uniontown Bible Church's, "The Living Room."

"As you read through the pages of this book you will sense and be captivated by the passion of Jeremy and Justin. I have had the privilege to know and experience Jeremy Willet and his music and message over the last

few years. His passion for the heart of God is contagious. I highly recommend this book to all."
—**Alan Greene**, Founder: LifeLight Communications, Inc.

"*carried.* will sweep you along on a journey toward intimacy with God. You gain a privileged and insightful view of the hearts and minds of some extraordinary Jesus-followers. Their passionate and gritty accounts of confronting poverty, injustice and brokenness celebrate God's power to transform lives, as we lay it all—the blessings and the pain—at the foot of the cross. Be prepared to be challenged toward cross-bearing, life-shaping worship and service to God."
—**Ben Homan**, President of Food for the Hungry.

"This book inspires me to look at each day a little closer and encourages me to ask myself an important question. Am I truly making good of the day that God has given? "This is the Day the Lord has Given, Let us Rejoice in It". The authors of *carried.* share how staying connected with God will inspire you to serve in a manner that pleases him."
—**Michael Jerke**, Avera Behavioral Health Center.

"There is no more powerful a life lived than one in passionate pursuit of Jesus Christ and the pursuit of sharing His life-changing love with a broken and needy world. I have seen this power and love displayed in the lives and ministry of Willet. These men have fallen deeper and deeper in love with Christ and as a result, His heart for the poor, the orphaned, the widowed, the sick and the needy has become their hearts. This book is a profound reminder that regardless of age, race, economic status, or gender we can all participate in the work the Lord is doing around the world."
—**Crystal Miller**, Columbine shootings survivor, author, and national speaker.

"People have a deep hunger that keeps them searching but many times remains a mystery. You will find your answer in the pages of this book. One of these chapters is specifically for you. Once you find it, keep reading because not only will this book be an eye opener, it will also inspire you to take it a step further."
—**Pam Plasier**, Mission Haiti Founder.

"As the body of Christ one of our crimes against humanity is our indifference and tolerance towards the world's problems we are faced with. This tolerance lulls us into a state of limbo that kills action. Without action there is no rescue. For some, without rescue there is no hope. You can be that hope. *carried.* is a story of two who are choosing to be exactly that."
—**Eric Samuel Timm**, International artist, communicator, author, www.nooneunderground.com

"*carried.* is a book that not only exposes the reality of the poor among us, but also challenges the reader to be a part of the solution in overcoming poverty. Having traveled with WILLET to Ethiopia and Haiti in 2009, I also witnessed first hand . . . how Christ carried us through villages of extreme poverty and created change in all of us that were present . . . *carried.* is a must-read."
—**Glen Willet**, Pastor of Quest Community Church.

carried.

carried.

Copyright © 2009 by Jeremy Willet and Justin Hanneken

Edited by George Fold IV
Graphics by Justin Willet

All rights reserved. **No part of this publication may be reproduced, stored in a retrieval system, or transmitted in any form or by any means, electronic, mechanical, photocopying, recording, or otherwise, without the prior permission of the authors.**

Scripture quotations are taken from the *Holy Bible: New King James Version* **(unless otherwise noted).**

Jeremy would like to thank: *Jesus, My wife Kathleen-mother to the motherless, our sponsored kids (Abeba, Mathewos, Meseret, Genet, and Arefayne), Mom & Dad, Mom2, Justin, Jordan, Caleb, my family, Quest Community Church, and WILLET friends.*

Justin would like to thank: *Jesus, Karena, Gloria (JOY to sad people) and Bryce (bringing Light to dark places). Thanks God for our sponsored kids: Bhavantha, Queljohn, Goytom and Sanbate. For George (who's been so patient with me through the editing process), Tommy T. who keeps me accountable, Dad who prays constantly for me, my mentors Pastor Gary Buchman and Dr. Tom Darner, my family, and the most amazing students I have ever met: tbc "engage" youth.*

Together, the authors would like to thank: *Jesus-thanks for carrying the cross; Food for the Hungry; WILLET; Mission Haiti; USAID; Pete Green; Justin Willet, Al, Jayme, and the folks at National Book Network; and all of our endorsers and contributors.*

For more information, please visit www.carriedbook.com.

ISBN: 978-1-61658-413-9

At the author's request, all royalties due to the authors will be forfeited and instead, distributed in the following ways:

45% • As an independent band, WILLET has adopted 3 villages in Africa, found sponsors for over 1000 orphaned children, launched a youth program called Hunger Strike, lead several international mission trips, and commissioned Jeremy's wife, Kathleen, as a full-time missionary to Haiti. WILLET MISSIONS exists to bring the love of Jesus Christ to those living in poverty through a partnership with *Food for the Hungry*, and will receive 45% of this book's proceeds.

45% • One of the greatest opportunities afforded Christian teenagers is to serve on international mission trips. Sadly, many teens do not answer the call due to a fear of not being able to raise the support money (plane ticket, in-country costs, etc.) For this reason, 45% of the proceeds gained from this book will go toward sending willing teens on mission trips to reach the nations for Jesus Christ through WILLET MISSIONS.

10% •Thanks to a matching grant through *Food for the Hungry* and *USAID*, every purchase of this book will send **$20** to support feeding programs, water sanitation, HIV/AIDS support, agricultural training, and conflict mitigation in Ethiopia, Congo, Kenya, Rwanda, Mozambique, Sudan, Burundi, Bolivia, and Haiti.

intro.	11
love.	15
blood.	25
forgiveness.	33
garments.	45
change.	61
kingdoms.	77
salt.	89
water.	101
epilogue.	115
study guide.	119

table of contents.

intro.

This book is a conversation.

Many will say the conversation is between one man that makes his living as an independent Christian artist, and another who makes his living as a youth pastor. The way we make our living is also our *way of life*, as we both have dedicated our lives to loving Jesus, loving the poor and hurting, and carrying the cross to a world in love with kingdoms. We will draw some conclusions for you of what we sense God calling "good" for us, but we challenge you to pray and ask God what conclusions He has for you. Some topics we will leave unresolved, because to us, they still remain as such.

Following a trip to Africa together in February of 2009, we began the writing process for carried. The majority of this book was written while we were both in separate places in the country (sometimes in the world) speaking, playing music, leading worship, coordinating mission projects and doing youth ministry. Sometimes we would write from a hotel room, backstage at a venue, in an airport, or at a local coffee shop. Other times, ideas for the book would come so quickly that we would exchange ideas via text messages until we had a chance to write from our computers.

When I (Jeremy) share about the love of Christ at WILLET concerts, I often say, "as a band, we don't have all the answers but we know the One who does, and we want to point you to Him." If the words on these pages point you to the Holy One whose story appears on the Greater Pages, then we have accomplished our goal. In the Holy Scriptures, you will find the bread of life. You will read about the One who paid it all, setting aside His glory to pick up and carry a cross of shame. You will learn of a God who wants to carry you along life's journey.

If we can journey with you, we'd consider it an honor and a privilege.

To share your thoughts and stories, and to **DOWNLOAD THE FREE SONG, *CARRY THE CROSS*, by WILLET,** please visit our website: www.carriedbook.com

love.

Take this book and turn it sideways.

Place your right hand on the right side of the blank page. Be sure to leave room for two hands. We know this seems silly, but try it.

Now, take a pencil, open your fingers slightly, and trace your right hand.

Now, switch hands, open your fingers slightly, and trace your left hand.

Good.

Now, take that same pencil, and on each "thumb", write the number 1.

On each finger following, number the remaining fingers in sequential order; 2-pointer, 3-middle, 4-ring, and 5-pinky.

You are doing so well.

Now, see the boxes below? Starting with the one on the left, write the letter, "F", then "G" in the next box, then "A", "B", "C", "D", and "E".

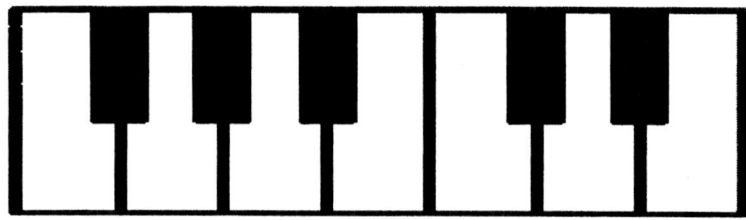

Congratulations! You have just completed your very first piano lesson! (A $20 value included at no extra charge- Our gift to you.) You are on your way to being a star!

We know you didn't buy this book to learn piano; however, there is a reason that you are reading this and it goes beyond an elementary lesson in piano theory. I (Jeremy) received my very first piano lesson from my Dad when I was seven years old. At the time, I didn't think piano books were the best gift for my seventh birthday, but with piano books come piano lessons, and thus my life in music began.

When a music teacher begins instructing a brand new student with no musical experience, a great way to start is by using something that they are already familiar with. Remember, in your first lesson all we asked you to do was:

    1. Draw your hand
    2. Number your fingers
    3. Write seven letters

Hopefully, this came natural to you, but imagine if that's all the further you ever went learning piano? Knowing just the fundamentals; using numbers and letters, would never allow you to experience the joy of playing a song. This exercise has some interesting parallels to Christianity. In most church services, aspects such as music, drama, pictures, stories, prayers and teaching are incorporated into the program. Although the music may sound a bit different then what we are used to hearing on the radio, and the drama is not quite "TV-ready," we feel a connection to parts of the service based on what we have been exposed to in real-life. This connection allows us to let our guard down enough to learn the "fundamentals" of Christianity.

If we can just be honest with each other, churches in America are all about comfort. Recently, while on vacation, I (Justin) visited a church in the Outer Banks, North Carolina. The pastor stood up and greeted the guests. He invited everyone to participate in the service as much as they could while "feeling comfortable." At least once a year in churches across America, that "comfortable" feeling is disrupted when we set aside a Sunday to recognize the cross. We discuss the love of our Savior and His sacrifice for our sins, but then quickly dismiss the reality of death on a cross with the story of resurrection. The resurrection of Christ is extremely important (1 Corinthians 15:13); however, Christ's death, and specifically, death on a cross, ultimately reveals something more: God's love.

Throughout your life, perhaps you have heard that God is love. Maybe someone told you that Jesus loves you or you sang songs about His love in Sunday school or junior church. Our question is, how do you really know? Most Christians reading this will immediately think of this verse:

This is love, that while we were yet sinners, Christ died for us.[1]

One day I (Justin) sat alone with the Lord. Have you ever done that? Have you ever just opened the Word of God and knew that He was present? He is always present.

So, I sat with the Lord and we talked about love. Actually, I talked. I said, **"God, I know You love me. I've felt it, and experienced it and I need to see it in Your Word."** Romans 5:8 came to mind immediately.

In our body, the flesh[2] is always present. Adam's sin is present as well, and for those who have trusted Christ, the Holy Spirit is present. Was the Holy Spirit the one that brought Romans 5:8 to the forefront of my mind? I'm not sure. I do know, however, that what happened several minutes later was from Him. Test it for yourself and see. Ask Him to reveal His will for your life, at this

---

[1] Romans 5:8

[2] Flesh—your flesh consists of your personal desires which are in opposition to God's will.

very moment, while you are reading this. What does God want to say to your heart?

Several years ago, I learned of a method of studying the Bible called First Mention. Rob Bell talks about First Mention in his book *Velvet Elvis*. As I was pondering the love of God and whether it was possible to see, from His Word, a new and clear, concise picture of His love, I was reminded of First Mention.

This technique of studying the Bible is quite simple and yet amazingly enjoyable. Think of a subject that you want to learn about and then reduce it to just one word. Next, search for the first place that the word appears chronologically in the Bible. In some cases, the word's first mention will reveal something unique about God. In other cases, it will relate back to the cross and the redeeming work of Jesus Christ. That's it! Simple, eh? Some people use a popular online bible search to find the word, and that's ok, but starting in the beginning and simply reading God's word is much more fun.

On this particular day, in this particular case, the word I was concerned with was *love*.

How long could this possibly take?

I was sure that the word *love* must show up in the Creation account somewhere. Nope. OK, well, the word must show up somewhere in the story of the first marriage and the first family? Nope. Alright, well, that's weird but I'll keep looking. Surely the story of Noah or the repopulating of the earth will yield a revolutionary find? You guessed it: double nope.

Twenty-two chapters into the book of Beginnings you find the first mention of this word love. Look it up for yourself: Genesis 22:2.

Then He [God] said [to Abraham], "Take now your son, your only son Isaac, the son whom you <u>love</u>, and go to the land of Moriah, and offer him there as

a burnt offering on one of the mountains of which I shall tell you."

Ok, what?

Are you serious?

The first place that the word love is mentioned in the Scriptures is in a verse about murder? Wait—this can't be. The first mention of love comes at the result of God requiring Abraham to sacrifice His promised son, the son whom he loves, as an offering to the Lord? Requiring Abraham to sacrifice Ishmael—now that I could understand, but Isaac? Something must be wrong here.

You probably know the story, but here's a quick precursor: Back in Genesis 17:1, the LORD appeared for the first time to 99-year-old Abraham. Not only does God show up and speak to Abe, He also presents a deal. A deal of massive implications! Abe's part: Walk blameless before the LORD. The LORD's part: Exceeding multiplication of Abraham's seed. Next, in Genesis 18, the LORD reveals that **Abraham will surely become a great and mighty nation and all the nations of the earth shall be blessed in him.**[3] Not only that, but God ponders if all of this is to be so, **Shall I hide from Abraham what I am doing?**[4] God always has a plan and He reveals His plan to whomever He chooses, whenever He chooses.

And now, back to Genesis 22. Let's look at verse 1.

Now it came to pass after these things that God tested Abraham and said to him, "Abraham!" And he said, "Here I am."

When the words, **"Here I am,"** appear in the Scriptures, specifically in the book of Genesis, this really means a lot more than just, "Hey, I'm right here." When a person says those words to the LORD, they are really saying to

---

[3] Genesis 18:18
[4] Genesis 18:17

God, "Here I am, and I'm ready to be obedient to what You would have me do." Can you say that to God? Did Abraham?

The story continues. In verse 3, we find out that Abraham arose early in the morning to accomplish this task of offering the son that he loves.

Early.

In the morning.

Abraham didn't put it off. He loved God and wanted to obey God. If you want to see the glory of God, you have to do what He says. So, Abraham, Isaac and a few servants set out for Mt. Moriah to do as the Lord had commanded them.

On the third day, Abraham sees the place where his son will meet his fate.

The third day.

And Abraham said to his young men, **"Stay here with the donkey, the lad and I will go yonder and worship and we will come back to you."**[5]

Wait a minute. Did you catch this? God was testing Abraham and the challenge put forth was to sacrifice the son that he loved. Abraham has made it this far and he tells his servants, "Wait here, we'll be back"—emphasis on WE! I thought Isaac had to die? Isaac was the offering and yet Abe tells his servants, "We will be back."

Why did Abraham bring the servants in the first place? There are some objects present: fire, a knife, and wood. In order for the wood to arrive at the altar, it had to be carried. Not by Abraham. Not by the servants, but by Isaac—the one whom the wood was intended for: The sacrifice.

---

[5] Genesis 22:5

"My father!" "Look, the fire and the wood, but where is the lamb for a burnt offering?"[6] Weren't you just hoping that Isaac would speak up and ask this question?

"God will provide,"[7] Abe says.

They reach the place.

The wood is ordered.

Isaac is bound.

On the wood that he himself carried.
On the mountain that God told them about.

Abraham stretched out his hand, and raised the knife.

God spoke: **Abraham! Abraham!**[8]

Abe's response? Here I am. The same response he gave back in v.1 of Ch. 22. The same response he gave Isaac in v. 7 of the same chapter.

Here I am. Ready, and willing, to do what God says.

God stops the offering. He provides a ram, caught in a thicket, as the substitutionary offering for Isaac.

Surely Abe is pleased.

God is pleased.

Isaac is, well, probably very pleased.

And God knows that Abraham fears Him.

In order to remember this, Abe names the place.

---

[6] Genesis 22:7
[7] Genesis 22:8
[8] Genesis 22:11

The-LORD-will-provide.

-or-

YHWH-Yireh.

So what does this amazing story have to do with the first mention of the word *love*?

Everything.

Roughly 2,000 years later, God took His Son, His only Son, the Son whom He loves, up on to a mountain.

He carried the wood, Himself.

An offering.

The Offering.

For your sins and mine.

There was no ram caught in the thicket that day at Mt. Calvary.

He is our Substitute, He is The Sacrifice.

Jesus Christ, the Lamb, died for the sins of the world, because God is love.

Here.

I Am.

What will you do with what He has done for you? Will you put your trust in Him?

Not just Savior. Not just Lord, but Savior and Lord of your life—now and forever. In Jesus' Name, Amen.

blood.

I (Jeremy) now have blood on my hands and I can't go back to where I was.

Growing up, I always had aspirations to become a musician and tour the world. I was born in February of 1985, and raised in a Christian home in Westminster, MD by my parents, Glen and Barbara Willet. My earliest memories recall getting ready for church, helping my dad by turning pages at the piano during the service, and attending Sunday school every week as a family. My mom has been a special education teacher for more than 25 years and my Dad taught piano before eventually starting a church in Taneytown, Maryland called, Quest Community Church.[1] I received Christ when I was almost four years old and began to follow in my father's footsteps of music and ministry. My parents had 2 other sons, Justin and Jordan, and growing up, we did everything together.

Just as I received piano books and piano lessons when I turned seven years old, the same applied to my brothers. As we grew up, we began to expand to other instruments such as bass, guitar and drums. We started writing some music together during summer break when our parents weren't home. We didn't own a drum kit at the time, so I would play the drum parts using a Roland synthesizer and electric piano, while Justin cranked up the distortion on his 15-watt Marshall amp, and Jordan sang into an unplugged microphone. After several rehearsals, we would set up "front-porch" concerts on the front deck of our log home for the neighborhood. No one ever came to these concerts (which now, looking back, I am totally fine with), but we were living the dream!

As I got a little older, I met some friends in middle school that were into Christian music and wanted to start a band. We began to write music after school and on the weekends, and at the age of 15 (2000), I announced to my family that I was the keyboardist and lead vocalist for the band *Superunknown*. At the time of my very first

---

[1] www.questcc.org

show, my uncle was in the middle of a long battle with cancer. I remember hearing how badly he wanted to attend my first concert, but we weren't sure if his body had enough strength to come out of the house. Our very first show was in an old Salvation Army building in Westminster, MD, and the room was full of our friends and family, including my Uncle Jim. After the concert, I remember seeing him walk slowly to his car, but stop to throw-up over a fence because of the chemotherapy treatments. Two weeks later, my Uncle Jim passed away. It was his first and last concert here on earth, but I know he has heard every song I've played since then from the best seat in the house.

Prior to my uncle getting sick, our family farm was struck by a tornado one cold, winter night. The following summer, a concert called "Barnstorm" was held on the property as the rebuilding of the barn was underway. I remember Uncle Jim saying,

"It appeared that Satan was trying to ruin our party . . . but he didn't."

Throughout my life, those words have always stayed with me.

After a few years, *Superunknown* began to fade away. Following the last show, I promised myself I would never start another band.

God had other plans.

After a few months of not playing music, I began to write worship music for the church. I began playing some of this music at coffeehouses, retreats and churches, and then I received a call to lead worship at a large Youth For Christ conference in NJ.

The requirements?

"Must have full worship band."

Around this time I noticed that Justin had never put

down his electric guitar, so I approached him about playing this one show with me. We assembled some other members to play the conference, but after the event, felt a great calling to keep playing music. After several months of playing weekend shows, we decided to make things a bit "more official" and called the band, *Clearview*. We began to tour regionally while juggling school and side jobs.

At this time in my life, I was teaching piano and finishing my Associates degree in Fine Arts from the community college. I rented a studio at a local music shop called *Coffey's Music* and taught 40 students each week. In one year, I was able to pay off my vehicle, rent an apartment, buy a brand new Taylor guitar and pay cash for an engagement ring. Life was good. My dreams were typical of a new artist. I wanted to land a record deal, win awards, hear my songs on the radio, go on big tours, and be recognized as a great musician and songwriter.

God had other plans.

In the first 5 years of my musical career, I rationalized that I was "carrying the cross" because I was writing Christian music, playing at churches, and ministering to teenagers. What I quickly realized however was that the "weight" I was carrying was not the cross, but rather my dreams. In 2006, I married my very first girlfriend, Kathleen, after dating for five years. We committed to a relationship of purity and, in fact, saved our very first kiss for the day that we got engaged to help remove sexual temptation. We now live together in a home in Westminster, Maryland but are following God's leading of my wife to full time missionary work in Haiti. It was also in 2006 that I decided to surrender my dreams as a musician and answer the call to full time ministry through music. This decision was not easy because it would require me to sell my vehicle, cancel all of my piano lessons, stop college education, travel without health insurance, and live off of $200 per month. This decision is what ultimately birthed what we now call WILLET, as Justin and Jordan also surrendered to the call of fulltime ministry and graduated early from high school to be able to tour full time. At the time, we didn't realize how God was molding the ministry of WILLET, but in 2007, our world was turned upside-down.

As a band, we boarded an airplane and traveled to Ethiopia, Africa with a Christian relief and development organization called, Food for the Hungry. When we landed in the capitol city, Addis Abeba, I remember seeing literally hundreds of children on a sidewalk with their hands outstretched. They were begging for food, water, medicine and clothing. We later learned that the sidewalk where these children were begging would also become their bed each night.

Orphans.

Orphaned because of the HIV/AIDS virus.

Orphaned because of unclean water.

Orphaned because of the lack of food.

Orphaned because they didn't have "enough."

As we continued through our 10-day trip, we visited the village that we would later adopt as a band called, Zeway.

Prior to this trip, my wife and I began sponsoring a girl from Zeway named, Abeba, which means "flower." We committed to support her for $32/mo. while also writing her letters and sending her photos. On this trip to Ethiopia, I had the opportunity to meet Abeba. I remember the first time I saw her. She greeted me through a translator and introduced me to her family. Then all of a sudden, she went running into her hut. She was gone for a few minutes and I began to wonder what she was doing. Is she playing with toys? Is this the last that I'll get to see her? I even began to get a little selfish thinking things like, "I just traveled thousands of miles to see you and I only got to spend one minute with you!" Abeba came back out of her hut and began walking towards me. In her hands she held a big stack of papers. Because she had been gone for a few minutes, I was trying to see what she was holding. As she got closer, I recognized something on the paper.

My handwriting.

Abeba wasn't in her hut playing with toys. She didn't have toys. She had a bed, small blanket and a container where she kept her letters safe. You see, Abeba clung to those letters as her source of hope because they were letters written in love. The letters told her that she was loved by God and loved by us. It was at this moment that I realized these children living in poverty are more than statistics, and they need our help.

Growing up, I remember hearing pastors and speakers get on stages and speak about missions, poverty, and hungry children. I recall leaving events frustrated after hearing them speak because they would always put emphasis on statistics. They would share that 6,500 children in Africa alone would be orphaned in one day from HIV/AIDS, and how 30,000 people every single day would die from hunger around the world.[2] Now, these statistics are true, but I remember thinking, "There is no way I can help 6,500 orphans! I wouldn't know where to start to try and feed 30,000 people around the world." Therefore, I left the events, and although I felt bad for the children, I did nothing.

God had other plans.

After holding the hands of orphans, wiping the blood from children's faces, visiting with HIV patients, and

---

[2] You are probably familiar with the time when Jesus fed 5,000 people at one time. Matthew 14:21 tells us that this number only counted the men, "besides women and children." Any time that we have heard preachers speak on this passage, they do the math that including women and children, somewhere between 25,000-**30,000** were fed at one time. Is it possible that 2,000 years ago Jesus was letting us know that there would come a time when 30,000 people would die each day due to hunger-related causes?

seeing the poverty that overwhelms Ethiopia, I knew we couldn't be silent. In a journal that we were keeping while on our trip, I wrote these words while sitting in a dirty hotel room in Zeway:

"If WILLET as a band never writes another song, goes on another tour, puts out another record, or becomes successful in the music industry's eyes, but one child in Africa is saved from the horror of poverty, then this whole thing was worth it."

That one child that we committed to as a band quickly became over 1000 as churches across America began to respond to the need. The next two years following this trip would be spent telling the stories of beautiful children from Ethiopia. A lot of people have picked up a cross and carried it around another country for a week or months at a time. Something happens though, when you carry a cross over 'there' and you bring a cross back as well. Several times at events, our stage time would be cut short because of scheduling issues, and we would have to choose between playing our songs or speaking on behalf of our mission work overseas. I'll never forget the commitment that our band made on the floor of that dirty hotel room; it's a cross that we cannot put down. The burden of "success" that I was previously carrying was now replaced with the cross, and every time, I would choose to carry the cross and speak on behalf of children that couldn't speak for themselves. I now have blood on my hands, blood of innocent children, and I can't go back to where I was.

forgiveness.

> ***"Maybe redemption has stories to tell, maybe forgiveness is right where you fell."***
> —**Switchfoot,** *from the song,* **"Dare You to Move"**

As a young boy, I (Justin) found myself staring up at a statue of a man on the cross. I knew how he got there, but I wasn't sure why he was still there. The bronzed figure wore a crown of thorns and a cloth around his mid-section. Week after week I was dragged to church. I hated it. I always believed in God's existence, but I did not know Him, nor did I want to know His Son. As I passed the figure, and/or the altar, (I'm not sure which) I was supposed to kneel and touch my forehead, chest, left shoulder, right shoulder.

Every.

Single.

Time.

For the first 17 years of my life, I went to church because I was forced to. My mom said it was the right thing to do. It was Mom, my brother, Matt, my sister, Krysten and I—every Sunday, week after week. The hardest part for me to deal with was that my dad never went with us. Dad got to sleep in, because he tended bar (for 19 years) and was up late the night before. During this time, I memorized the prayers, confessed my countless sins to the priests, lit the candles, ate the wafers, drank the wine, admired the statues and heard the stories. Stories are a huge part of life, as I am sure you are aware. Sitting in that church during those years, I found the only place in the world where the stories did not make any sense to me. I'm not sure why, but the leadership in that place encouraged you not to read the Great Storybook. We were only supposed to hear it read and explained from those who wore the robes and were "holy."

When I was in elementary school our family went on vacation. This was a yearly event and something that I always looked forward to. Sitting at a beach house, on the

Jersey Shore, an evangelist came on the TV. He carried a passionate message to his viewers. I do not know who he was, and I'm not sure what he was saying. I didn't watch him—but, my dad did. Not only did he watch, but he got convicted by something that was said.

That day, my world collapsed.

After hearing the evangelist's words, my dad went to my mom and told her that he was having an affair on her. He had another woman in his life and he didn't want to be with my mom anymore.

At that time, true hatred rose up in my heart.

I remember the days that followed—the tears that were spent, as my dad left us to go be with his new love. I hated my dad. I told my mom these words: "As long as I live, I will never forgive that man for what he has done to our family."

My mom, Betsy, God bless her, tried to salvage the broken relationship. She offered counseling and did everything she could to take my dad back. He wanted none of it. He moved on.

Back in 1990, things were different than they are in 2009. None of my friends' parents were divorced and it wasn't something that was nearly as prevalent as it is today. I felt alone, abandoned and discouraged. This led me to a new group of friends and a new lifestyle. Underage drinking, partying, and theft became my new obsessions. When I was 15 years old, I got a job at my Uncle's bar. I began drinking and stealing liquor and food. After about a year of this, I decided one night to join some friends and try to steal some car stereos.

At 1am that morning, we were arrested.

I called my mom to bail me out of jail, and she was not happy.

I had a lot of problems in my life at that time. What was Mom's solution? Confirmation classes.

For the better part of the next year, I went, because I had to. I didn't have a choice. The ultimatum was stated. If I went, my grandfather (we called him Pop-pop), who loved me, would pay for my college. If I didn't go, I was on my own.

I continued the classes, and I continued to party. Week after week went by. Sometimes I went to class, other times I'd skip and go play pool. The times when I did show up, I found myself asking questions. I don't remember exactly what they were trying to teach me. I also do not remember what questions I asked, but I remember getting bogus answers. I was often told not to ask 'those' kind of questions in that place. I wanted answers.

Around the time that the classes were ending, something very strange happened. I never made it to the confirmation ceremony. The date and the location were set as family came in from out of town for this momentous event. I had just gotten my license and my first car. I set out early that morning with the intent of graduating. I wore my suit, my girlfriend, Karena, was with me, and we got in the car heading for a huge cathedral at Charles St. in Baltimore. Anticipating the meal and celebration afterwards, we headed off, only to end up lost—seriously lost. We drove around Baltimore for over 2 hours looking for the place and could not find it. Finally, we got directions and made it there, just as the celebration was ending. People I knew from the class came walking out with their families and friends, rejoicing and celebrating. And there I was: the disappointment. What they were celebrating, I still do not know, but I was faced with frowns, ridicule, and disgust. Imagine driving several hours to see someone do something that you think is important for them, and then they don't show up to be a part of it. What a waste of time.

A short time after that, another very peculiar event occurred. A friend from high school, named Ben Hickok, showed up at my house one day, and he was carrying a cross. He dragged it up the driveway, the front steps and let it rest right there in my mom's living room. I greeted Ben, "Oh, wow, what are you doing here? I haven't seen you in two years?!" Ben graduated High School before I did. He was one of my good friends and I really looked up to him. Ben played drums better than I did; was a better mountain biker and had the attention of the girl that I wanted to date. Nevertheless, I was so excited to see Ben—that is, until he spoke.

Ben looked me in the eye and said these words:
"How is your relationship with Jesus Christ?"

That was Ben's cross that he bore to me, Chuck, Dave, Cary, Brad and all of his old friends. We hadn't seen Ben in two years, and it turns out he went to Bible College. He fell in love with the Savior that he once met when he was younger and he picked up a cross for the first time in his life.

Given my history with religion, Ben's message was not received well. I told him that I believed in God, went to church, and that was enough for me. He left my mom's house that day and I wanted nothing to do with him.

About a week later, he returned. Same cross, same conversation, same rejection. He left.

Another week went by, and he came back. Same cross, same conversation, different response. "Ben, I don't know what your deal is, but I just want to hang out with you again," I said. His response, "Great, let's hang out." That week was intense. I went out to dinner with Ben's discipleship group, played basketball with his friends, and was welcomed at his church. This place was different. The people cared about me. They wanted to be there! They wanted me there! Interestingly, at this church, there were no statues, no candles, no priests, and the man on the cross was no longer on the cross. I heard a message about Him being raised from the dead!

That week, in 1999, shortly before graduating high school, I heard the Savior's Good News for the first time.

I understood the cross and the resurrection. Ben walked me through 'the Romans Road,' a method of sharing the Good News of Jesus Christ with someone using verses from Romans.[1]

I prayed to God for the first time. I was praying through His Son Jesus Christ, asking Him to forgive and to save me. Do you know that God does not hear the prayers of sinners? I know this is going to be a little bit hard for you to swallow, but check out John 9:31.[2]

So, that day, in 1999, Jesus came into my life as my Savior and Lord. He had been wooing me, trying in so many ways to get my attention, to wake me up, and He gave His servant Ben a cross to bear, a cross with my name on it.

After trusting Christ at 17, I knew that I was saved. Life was different. My behaviors didn't change over night, but I began to love the things that God loves and hate the things that He hates. My own sin became evident as Ben took the time to disciple me. We walked through the Bible, and I learned the truth of God's word. I still had yet to pick up a cross, but I started to make changes in my life.

God caused me to despise cursing. I used to use the F-bomb without any thought or concern, and I could no longer say it. I couldn't take God's name in vain, and I could no longer listen to music that did. I stopped watching certain movies and, only by His grace, I stopped drinking alcohol and looking at pornography. One by one, Jesus Christ Himself took away all of my sin. He delivered me from addiction and showed me that my life had meaning and purpose.

---

[1] Romans 3:23, 5:12, 6:23, 10:9.

[2] The first prayer that God hears is the sinner's prayer of repentance. The literal Greek of John 9:31 reads: **"We know and that sinful ones God not hears, but if anyone is God-fearing is, and the will of him does, this one He hears."** Proverbs 15:29 agrees with this. Acts 19:13-16, Psalm 18:41, Psalm 34:15, Psalm 66:18 all support our conclusion as well.

There was a cross for me to bear and I didn't even know it yet.

Shortly after trusting Christ, I went to, my girlfriend, (and now wife and mother of our 2 beautiful girls) Karena's house to witness to her. I brought my Bible and had my verses picked out. That night, we had the worst fight we've ever had. I told her that if she didn't trust Christ, she was going to burn in Hell. I was familiar with how to be saved, but had yet to understand grace, love, or mercy. As we fought and cried, her parents were scared. Only by God's grace, we didn't break up that night, but I did make a deal with God. I told Him that I really wanted to be with Karena, but I would leave her if He told me to. I was hearing His voice and it was amazing, and I said, "Lord, I will leave this girl for You. Just say the word. I will not marry her, Lord, unless she trusts You as her Lord and Savior."

During college, I got involved in several campus ministries. At Anne Arundel Community College, God led me to a group called Baptist Student Ministries. For a new Christian, this was a great place to grow. It was with AACC's BSM that I went on my first Christian retreat, and my first mission trip. It was there that I first sang to God, first ministered to and discipled others.[3] From there, I graduated and went to University of Maryland Baltimore County. At UMBC, I got involved in just about every Christian group on campus. I grew the most while involved in Intervarsity Christian Fellowship. I am also greatly indebted to all that God taught me through the Passion Movement and Louie Giglio.[4] During college, Karena got involved in these Christian groups as well. We went to concerts, retreats and various churches together. It was at a BSM retreat for college students, that Karena surrendered her life to Jesus Christ. Jami Smith led worship and during her singing time, she shared the Gospel. It made sense to Karena for the first time! When asked about her conversion, she'll tell you the story, and

---

[3] Random tidbit for the day: Microsoft Word hates whenever the word disciple is used as a verb.
[4] www.268generation.org

she'll also tell about the godly women in her life that carried a cross to her as well (Thanks God for Becky, Annie, and Maria).

Shortly after Karena got saved, we got engaged.

Around this time, God was doing another great work in my heart. He taught me about grace and revealed the un-forgiveness that I harbored in my heart against my dad. God also told me that "He and I couldn't move forward until I forgave my dad." At my Lord's prompting, I released my dad from the chains of my own unforgiveness, and was subsequently released from the hatred that I harbored toward him as well. Not only that, but God saved Dad as well through a completely different situation, place and time. As we both became born again[5] in Jesus, our relationship was born again as well.

During one BSM meeting at UMBC, our campus minister told us about a youth conference that was coming to town and looking for volunteers to help out. He said, "If anyone isn't doing anything this weekend, and would like to show up and help, please do." I agreed immediately! This sounded like fun and any place that Christians were gathering is where I wanted to be. Besides, how much work could it really be?

I showed up at the BCM/D's Youth Evangelism conference ready to serve. Certain I'd be selling CD's, parking cars, and handing out T-shirts and info, I approached a worker there. I introduced myself and told them my intent. They said, "Great, you'll help counsel teens at the altar call tonight."

What?

Me?

I had never cared much for teenagers; they actually really got on my nerves. I also had little to no confidence

---

[5] John 3:3 and 3:7

in leading someone to know Christ, and wasn't convinced I could learn how to do it in just a few hours. I got back in my car and considered driving away because of fear. I know now that God was pursuing me, once again, as He had all along.

I went back into the conference, and later that night, I found myself sitting face to face with a 12-year-old boy. His parents had just gotten divorced and he struggled with the same things that I did as a pre-teen. This was surreal. We cried and prayed together and he rededicated his life to Christ. I'm not sure how much that moment meant to that 12-year-old boy, nor do I know his name. I know, however, exactly how much it meant to me. It was in that moment I heard God speak loud and clear:

"You are going to be ministering to students for the rest of your life."

What?

Me?

God knows what He is doing, and He is completely in control. That day, at that student evangelism conference, God set a cross down right in front of me. He gave me an option: take it or leave it? How could I leave it? Peter says, **"To whom else shall we go Lord?"**[6]

The cross that Jesus had for me to carry was a cross to teenagers. Bill Hybels talks about each Christian having a "holy discontent." I wanted to let teenagers know that they did not have to die and go to hell.

At present time, I've been carrying this cross for 6 years. I've never put it down and only by His grace, I've never wanted to. Throughout this time, God has directed me to many places to which I have carried this cross: Taneytown, North Carolina, New York, *Creationfest*, Purple

---

[6] John 6:68

Door, Mexico, Guatemala and, most recently, Ethiopia with WILLET. God has given our family a passion for the nations and is teaching us what it means to live for others.

In 2006, Karena told me that her sister was going to get married in Mexico. My response was, "I will never go to Mexico. Everyone who goes there ends up getting sick and coming home sick." Since proclaiming that, I've been to Mexico 7 times—5 for mission trips. Don't tell me that God doesn't have a sense of humor!

On one of the mission trips to New York, Lake Placid specifically, I made some new friends from Faith Baptist Church (Glen Burnie, MD). One of them, Jeff Higgins, said "Hey bro, pray for me after this trip is over, I'm going to apply for a worship leader position at a church in Taneytown." Having never even heard of the place before, I agreed to pray.

Two days after the trip, I called Jeff to ask how the interview went. He said, "Not well, dude. It just wasn't the right fit for me or them, but I gave them your name."

What?

Me?

I said, "Jeff, what'd you go and do that for? I'm no worship leader." He said, "Justin, not for worship, but for youth, God has called you to work with youth, hasn't He?" Of course He had. For over 2 years, I was patient in waiting for His timing. I never once applied to work as a youth pastor, or sought out a position, God simply ushered me into one.

He gave me a cross to bear for the teenagers of Taneytown and the surrounding areas. He also gave Karena a cross for the exact same kids.

Fast-forward six years, hundreds of new relationships (with us and more importantly with Jesus) and thousands of stories later, here we are.

Have you ever helped someone move furniture? It's an interesting task. I've always said that you can figure out who your true friends are when you see who shows up to help you move. Anyway, if you do help someone move, there comes a point where you go to lift something as a group: a washer, refrigerator, or dining room table. So you find yourself lifting with others, but you realize you are not actually lifting any weight. Perhaps you are the fourth man on a 3-man lift, or perhaps the weight of the object does not require your strength in the place you are standing. The cross we bear is like that. It has gotten heavy at times but it's never once been unbearable. Jesus is doing all the carrying, actually, it's when we try to lift on our own that things don't work out.

garments.

> *"Jesus now has many lovers of His heavenly Kingdom, but few bearers of His cross."*
> —Thomas A. Kempis

In three of the four Gospels, we read these words of Jesus:

If anyone desires to come after Me, let him deny himself, and take up his cross, and follow Me.[1]

When Jesus says this, it sounds appealing to us. From what we have learned, and what preachers have told us, this challenge to us makes sense. He must require something more than easy-believe-ism. He must be interested in something more than a Get-out-of-Hell-Free prayer. In Luke's Gospel, this verse contains an extra word that appears after cross. The word is: daily.

A cross.

Taken up.

Daily.

In June of 2009, WILLET was on THE 500 FACES TOUR traveling from Iowa to Ohio for Alive Festival. We had just completed a few festivals in Iowa with Decemberadio and Scott Krippayne, and were getting ready for the 15 hour drive to Alive when we noticed it was time for us to get an oil change on our van that had 200,000 miles on it. As we were talking to a few people at the festival, a gentleman named Cory explained that he was a mechanic and offered to help. The next day, we brought our van to his shop and he changed the oil, looked over the levels and even changed the windshield wipers. When we offered to pay him for his work, he declined and told us that he used his lunch shift to help us so that he was not using company time. We gave him a WILLET T-shirt instead, and thanked him for his servant's heart.

---

[1] Matthew 16:24, Mark 8:34, Luke 9:23

This story about Cory may not seem "revolutionary" by any means, but it does reveal a great message to all Christians. You see, Cory attended our concert and heard us talking about orphans overseas in places like Ethiopia, Rwanda and Uganda. During our talk, we always emphasize the need for us, as the Christian community, to use our God-given gifts to help others. The beauty of the body of Christ is that we all look different. Each of us has something to offer (on a domestic and international level), and Cory had his skills to assist a band that spends over 200 days per year on the road. We don't know Cory well, but by his heart and his actions, we sense that he is acquainted with the lifestyle of cross-carrying. His 1/2-hour of service to our ministry will not be forgotten.

The question remains: What did Jesus' words about cross-carrying mean to the first hearers?

Crosses in the 1st Century were reserved for criminals. They were built for enemies of the State (or empire). Shane Claiborne and Chris Haw, in their book *Jesus for President*, define the cross as "willingly suffering at the hands of the powers . . . an execution tool of the state that killed Jesus and countless insurgents."[2] So, what does bearing a cross mean for us?

Carrying the cross represents a lifestyle—one of putting to death our desires, and will, and following after Jesus, His desires and His will.

Claiborne and Haw challenge us to "be cautious not to abuse the idea of 'bearing our cross.'"[3] "The cross is too easily turned into a religious metaphor for any of our hardships. But the Bible never waters down the cross into a mere symbol that can make us feel more spiritual by wearing it around our necks."[4] When we think about what bearing a cross really means, we sense that doing

---

[2] Claiborne and Haw. *Jesus for President,* (Grand Rapids, Michigan: Zondervan, 2008). p. 277-78.
[3] Ibid.
[4] Ibid.

something for Jesus that leaves you tired, beat up and exhausted must have something to do with it.

Francis Chan echoes this idea, in his book: *Forgotten God*. Chan says, "Taking up my cross" has become a euphemism for getting through life's typical burdens with a semi-good attitude. Yet life's typical burdens—busy schedules, bills, illness, hard decisions, paying for college tuition, losing jobs, houses not selling, and the family dog dying—are felt by everyone, whether or not they follow the Way of Jesus."[5]

I (Justin) will never forget the first week that I began interviewing for the youth pastor position that I currently hold. Pastor Gary and I were alone in his office and he quoted an Old Testament scripture to me: "Justin, **Jesus was 'a man of sorrows acquainted with much grief.'** [6] "If you choose to accept this youth pastor position, you will be following after Him and this verse will become true of you at times. Are you sure that you want to be in youth ministry?'" Looking back, I know now that what Pastor Gary was asking me was whether I was willing to bear the cross of Jesus. Bearing a cross has to do with a lifestyle marked by living the way He lived and dying the way He died. Is that even possible? What was His death all about anyway?

There is an interesting verse that jumps off the page in 1 Timothy 4:10.

Through the leading of the Holy Spirit, Paul says to Timothy,

For to this end, we both labor and suffer reproach, because we trust in the living God, who is Savior of all men, especially to those who believe.

---

[5] Chan. *FORGOTTEN GOD*, (Colorado Springs, Colorado: David C. Cook, 2009). p. 124-25.
[6] Isaiah 53:3

The cross of Jesus Christ is about the living God. It is about love. It is about salvation. The salvation of **all men:**

Is He the Savior of the Jews? Yes.
The Gentiles? Yes.
People in Heaven right now? Yes.
People in Hades right now? Yes.[7]

1 Timothy 4:10 says that He is the Savior of all men, especially to those who believe.

In the very next verse, Paul tells Timothy to teach this faithful saying to others. The cross is about salvation for everyone who chooses Jesus as Savior and Lord. The cross is about Jesus defeating death. The cross is about the true Love of God being poured out through His own Son's blood so that sinners can be saved.

Is that all that it is about?

The cross is about community. It is a fellowship of suffering for all who believe. It is God's invitation into His Royal Family where you become a king and priest forever.[8] In God's community, there is always room at the table and there is more than enough food.[9] Do you know that God never intended you to live life alone? You might say, 'Well, what about singleness, didn't God say that some are to remain single for the work of the ministry?' Yes, He did make this clear, and yes, we have read 1 Corinthians 7:32-35. When we say that He never intended you to live life alone, we are talking about how He specifically created you to live in community with others.

---

[7] The very reason that they are in Hades is that they died in their sin, having not put their faith and trust in Jesus as Savior and Lord of their lives. He died to save them, but they have passed into eternity without salvation. Sadly, Hell will be their final place for all eternity.
[8] Revelation 1:5-6
[9] Isaiah 25:6

Think of Adam's beginning in Eden. Good man. Good existence. Good garden. Holy God. These are ALL adjectives that God chose to use. In fact, when the whole deal is done, God calls His creation **very good**[10]. At the end of Ch. 2, we find out that God has a further creation that He introduces to the situation. He says,

The LORD God said, "It is not good for the man to be alone. I will make a helper suitable for him.[11]
For the first time, since eternity past, God has now introduced that something is not good. This has major implications that we were created for relationship. Even when the Creator and the created are able to communicate and interact, God still determines that a helper is suitable for Adam. Interesting!

Look back at the first verse we quoted in this chapter: 1 Timothy 4:10. Notice the use of the words **we** and **all**. When Paul says that we labor and suffer reproach, he is speaking of people who are bearing and carrying crosses together. Whether crosses represent burdens for others' salvation, a desire to see God's economics carried out to the world—or both—together is the way that crosses are intended to be carried.

Simon and Andrew.

James and John.

Paul and Timothy.

Paul and Silas.

Jesus and Simon, Andrew, James, John, well . . . basically everyone He encountered.

Everyone who takes Jesus' command to "take up your cross" seriously is going to need some help. In the above statement, you'll notice the names of four of His first fol-

---

[10] Genesis 1:31
[11] Genesis 2:18 NIV

lowers. He spent three years with them teaching them what it looked like to die daily, take up their cross, and follow Him.

This brings us to the discussion of garments.

When we hear the word garments, the first thing that comes to mind is probably clothing, but this is the discussion of spiritual garments—clothing that God wants every Christian to wear.

The first and most important type of garment that can be worn by anyone who chooses is the garment of righteousness. This garment is imputed[12] when we put our trust in His atoning[13] work: the shed blood of Jesus Christ and in His resurrection. This garment was made available to us through His cross, which He bore, for us, bringing salvation to all who believe.

Look at the words of Isaiah 61:10, they make this point much better than we can:

I will greatly rejoice in the LORD, My soul shall be joyful in my God; For He has clothed me with the garments of salvation, He has covered me with the robe of righteousness, As a bridegroom decks himself with ornaments, And as a bride adorns herself with her jewels.

Notice here how God has Isaiah equate the robe of righteousness with the garb that would be worn at a wedding!

---

[12] Imputed: The righteousness of Christ is put on our account, as God considers Christ' death on our accord—thus we trade all of our sin for His righteousness, the greatest gift ever given.

[13] Atoning: the state of being reconciled to God. Because of the death of Christ, we can be at-one with God because God is satisfied with His Son's death on our behalf as the payment for our sins.

Then, in Matthew's version of the wedding parable, Jesus says:

But when the king came in to see the guests, he saw a man there who did not have on a wedding garment. So he said to him, 'Friend, how did you come in here without a wedding garment?' And he was speechless.[14]

In order to be with God, in Heaven, we must overcome death. The only way that we can do this is by embracing His substituionary death on the cross: on our behalf.

The cross is about community.

As we carry the cross, another type of garment that God wants us to be clothed in is the garment of accountability.

Brothers and sisters.

Surrounding us.

In community.

Bearing crosses.

Together.

For about three years, Jesus Himself had a garment, the twelve apostles. He surrounded Himself with them. Jesus had a group within the twelve that some preachers call "the inner circle."

The three.

Peter, James, and John were Jesus' inner garment. They were closer than the rest and He taught them some of the deeper truths of God.

---

[14] Matthew 22:11-12

Why would Jesus, being the Son of God surround Himself with this community of men? Was it for His sake? Certainly not, it was for their sake and the sake of the Gospel. These were the ones that Jesus would use to "be witnesses for [Him] in Jerusalem, Judea, Samaria and to the ends of the earth."[15]

Often times when we think of the community that Jesus experienced with the twelve, we tend to focus on their perspective. We say things like, "What must it have been like for them when Jesus went to the cross" and "What would they do now, would they just go back to their old jobs?" Our question is, what about Jesus' perspective? When Jesus went to the cross, the disciples were the ones who scattered just as the Scriptures said they would.

John 19:23 tells us that Jesus on the cross, was naked. His clothes, which had obviously been bloodied, were taken from Him. Also, His tunic was taken. The tunic is the inner garment. Our friend Patrick Kenney III has taught us a lot about garments. He says that this type, the tunic was valuable, made by the mothers of sons who are acknowledged as rabbis in their communities. Notice what the verse says, it was without seam, woven from the top in one piece. Patrick says, "Seamless stood for no area of life seen or unseen was motivated by agendas that did not have their source in God."

Another mention of "tunic" is found in Luke 3:11 where we find John saying,

The man with two tunics should share with him who has none, and the one who has food should do the same.

If a tunic in scripture was something similar to a long undershirt, this verse was emphasizing that they didn't need two undergarments, and the extra should be given to one in need.

---

[15] Acts 1:8

In addition, we find some of the very last words of Jesus quite interesting. Follow us here. Jesus says to his earthly mother, Mary:

Woman, behold your son! [John] Then He said to the disciple, "Behold your mother!" And from that hour that disciple took her to his own home.[16]

As the Son of God died, He arranged for His mother to be cared for by John. Remember, John was one of the three that He kept closest to Himself and some even believe that John was a relative of Jesus. This very act models for us the importance of caring for others (our mothers specifically). In addition to this, He died with no earthly possessions, everything was given away, stripped from Him and that's the way He wanted it. This reminds us of one-way missionaries that we have heard stories about. These followers of Jesus packed all that they own into a coffin and head to another country to carry a cross for Jesus. They go in this manner because they know that they are not coming back. For Jesus sake, they give their entire lives away even unto death.

In addition to giving ourselves away, the closest brothers and sisters in Christ that we surround ourselves with are our inner garment, or garment of accountability and we are to remain seamless for one another. What do we mean by seamless? Well, without fault and without blemish.

If you are having a hard time following us on the subject of garments, check out these verses from Hebrews 12:14-17.

Pursue peace with all people, and holiness, without which no one will see the Lord: looking carefully lest anyone fall short of the grace of God; lest any root of bitterness springing up cause trouble, and by this many become defiled; lest there be any fornicator or profane person like Esau, who for one morsel

---

[16] John 19:26-27

of food sold his birthright. For you know that afterward, when he wanted to inherit the blessing, he was rejected, for he found no place for repentance, though he sought it diligently with tears.

Holiness is much easier pursued in community and accountability with another brother or sister. If we surround ourselves with people who are not in pursuit of God's Way of living, we can become defiled by them. I (Justin) have seen this time and time again in teenage-relationships. Often times, students will enter into relationships with un-believers and qualify their behaviors as evangelism-dating, but too often they do not persuade the other person to follow Christ, but are rather persuaded to leave their once thriving relationship with Christ behind. The Hebrews 12 commentary on Esau found here reminds us that we must flee from fornication and profane living, or as the NIV Bible version puts it: "sexual immorality and godless" living.

For example, I (Justin) claim Jeremy as one member of my inner garment. I am to remain seamless (holy) for the sake of my testimony and for the sake of Jeremy's testimony. What if I don't? What if Jeremy claims me to be part of his garment and I go home, get drunk, cheat on my wife, and give myself a bad name – what have I done? I've given Jeremy a bad name too because people will see me and say, "I can't believe Jeremy is associated with that drunkard, adulterer, etc." I've also given the other two brothers in my garment, Jimmy Akers and Marc Duckworth, bad names too. If that's not troubling enough, I've also given God a bad name! In case no one has ever told you, God HATES to be misrepresented!

In 2007, I (Jeremy) was invited to travel on a 15-city tour in the Midwest by Food for the Hungry to speak on behalf of orphaned children. Just a few months prior, I had returned from my first trip to Ethiopia and I was excited to share my heart about the children.

In order to protect those individuals involved in the next event that I share with you, I will leave the name of the headlining band out of the story. Midway through the tour, we had an off day. I remember riding in the bus and looking at a map to find the location of the next tour date. From where we were the night before, the drive to the next city should have taken about four hours. Eight hours later, the bus stopped at a hotel, and the tour manager explained that we were heading downtown at 8pm. Because of the off day, the headlining band had requested to drive four hours off the route so they could go to a bar where they would not be seen by potential concert fans. The band offered to pay the tab and invited the whole tour to a tavern.

About one year prior to this, my wife and I vowed to not drink alcohol. We didn't feel as though the consumption of alcohol was a sin, but we would often open our home for small group studies and we never wanted a few drinks to become a stumbling block for our unsaved friends. Therefore, I declined the offer to join the tour at the bar that evening, and instead went to a restaurant and watched the MLB playoffs. When it was time for bus call (2 a.m.), I walked back to a bus full of some of the biggest names in Contemporary Christian Music completely drunk. I was embarrassed to even be on the same bus with them, because I knew that anyone that saw our group could easily associate the entire tour, Christian music, and even worse, Jesus, with the actions of our tour.

WILLET, as a band, is definitely not perfect, nor do we claim to be. We do, however, hold high standards of integrity because we are in front of thousands of young people each month, and we want our lives on and off stage to reflect Christ. Currently, we have a daily band devotion that is emailed to us by our Dad (and band pastor), Pastor Glen Willet. We use this time to learn from scripture, challenge each other with questions, and pray for each other. Sometimes the prayers are specific to the ministry of the band and other times they are concerning our personal lives. In addition, we also have rules in place for where we sign autographs on fans. We always sign the back of T-shirts and never sign pants above the knee. Finally, we honor a "buddy system" when going to the van and never allow fans to enter the vehicle. This eliminates the possibility of any situations or temptations that would not be pleasing to God. I have fired musicians in the past over issues such as underage drinking, smoking (after being told it was not permissible), sex outside of marriage, and pride. I will not tolerate the association with one member of our band to potentially ruin the mission that we started out to pursue. This, unfortunately, is not the "industry standard" in Christian music, but then again, WILLET is not playing music to fit into some cute industry box full of hypocrites. My prayer is that God will receive the glory through the rules we have in place. This is not about legalism, this is about righteousness.

Do you have a garment of accountability?

Your accountability garment is three people that are on the same page as you spiritually. Three people (we believe they should be the same gender) who want to pray with you, worship as you worship, seek God as you seek God, love others as you love others—if someone is not a Christian they can not be in your garment. You and your three should remain seamless and without blemish for each other and for the Lord Jesus.

We know that God does not want our garment to be defiled[17]. Check out Revelation 3:4:

You have a few names even in Sardis who have not defiled their garments; and they shall walk with Me in white, for they are worthy.

In this specific church (Sardis), we are given a picture of the amount of people who do not defile their garments. Only a few—the Bible says, ***a handful***. There is a verse in James Ch. 1 that you have probably heard quoted so many times. It says, ***"Pure and undefiled religion before God and the Father is this, to look after or-***

---

[17] Defiled: stained or contaminated by sin. Acts such as adultery or viewing pornography are sins that cause a person to not be living in purity before God.

phans and widows in their distress . . ."[18] We love this verse, we agree with it, we try to embody it, but we have one problem with people constantly quoting it: they leave off the last 8 words. We challenge you to put this book down and without reading on, can you tell us what the last 8 words of James 1:27?

Can you?

They are:

And to keep oneself unspotted from the world.

The Greek word for *unspotted,* literally means, "unblemished physically or morally." Sins and vices defile us. The company we keep can defile us. God's call for us is to remain above reproach. That is what we are talking about when we encourage you to have a garment of accountability. So, Jesus says, **be holy, for I am holy.**[19] Do you take Him seriously? Is this principle taught in your church? Is it important to the people that you consider your closest friends? Are you a person whose garment is tainted because of your actions or because you have allowed the misconduct of others influence you? The good news is that our God is in the business of making garments whiter than snow! God is in the *Clorox* business.

Now, we are going to do another activity together.

Begin to think on God.

Ask Him: who on this earth is thirsty like me? When we say "thirsty," we mean that you have a certain yearning for God, His ways, and His judgments. Jesus said in Matthew 5:6, **blessed are those who hunger and thirst for righteousness, For they shall be filled.** With that in mind, are you thirsty for God? Does anyone

---

[18] James 1:27
[19] 1 Peter 1:16

you know exhibit the same level of yearning for God as you do?

Ask Him: "Who is pursuing You in the way that I'm pursuing You?"

As each person comes to mind, write them down. If you are struggling, just look in your cell phone at the Christians that you call the most.

Write down 3 names.

<u>My Garment (people who are thirsty)</u>

1. _____
2. _____
3. _____

Your next challenge is to pray for these three. After praying, call them. Explain to them that they are in your garment and what that means. Chances are, they have never heard about this before. As time goes on, your garment will change. That's okay. Our point is that regardless of who is in your garment, you were not meant to live this life alone.

You were not meant to carry the cross alone.

change.

> Hey Jeremy—
>
> We gave your music a listen, and in the light of all the new things we're working on for now and next year, it just didn't feel like something we could devote any of our energies or resources to . . . something that you should obviously expect from any music company that would partner with you.
>
> It's been great meeting you guys and we have great respect and admiration for what you've been able to accomplish, by God's grace, without any real industry support. While we don't feel like the music is a fit for us and our roster, please let us know if there are any other ways we can help.
> Thanks again.
> Blessings—
> A&R Department @ Centricity Records

In an interview with K-Love radio in South Dakota on the Day of Fire / John Reuben / WILLET tour in 2009, I (Jeremy) was asked to describe what WILLET's "big break" was.

"Big break?" I asked. "If we received a big break, someone forgot to tell me."

Rejection letters like the one above, although respectfully submitted, are tough to receive. Since our start in 2006, WILLET has always kept the band logistics in-house. Justin designs all the merchandise, creates and maintains the website and produces all the promotion material and music videos.[1] Jordan is in charge of social networks, promotional and the street-team. My role in WILLET involves booking shows, coordinating mission trips, managing finances, leading rehearsals, writing songs, and planning the tour routings. In addition, I serve on a volunteer basis as the worship director at Quest Community Church, while also speaking at major

---

[1] www.willetonline.com

festivals and tours, and writing/recording devotions and pod-casts for Food for the Hungry. As a band, we strongly believe in the words of 1 Timothy 4:12:

Don't let anyone look down on you because you are young, but set an example for the believers in speech, in life, in love, in faith and in purity.

In the Christian Music industry, many bands rise to success with a hit radio single or top-selling album. Following that success, they will begin headlining major festivals and tours. At the height of their career, you may notice your favorite artist begin to stand behind a specific "cause." Some artists start their own organization; while others speak on behalf of one they feel passionate about. I am thankful for the lives that have been changed by artists in the Christian community that use their success to impact others.

In the first four years as a band, we sold 10,000 copies of our independent releases. We were able to set up online worldwide distribution and because of that, WILLET has had the opportunity to appear on national tours with Sanctus Real, Day of Fire, John Reuben, and major festivals with bands like *Switchfoot, Skillet,* and *Newsboys.* While on the road, we would spend time with up-and-coming bands that asked questions like:

"How do I make it like you guys?" "How do I get on big tours?" "How do I begin to make music a full time career?"

There was a time when I would answer these questions by giving some advice that we learned over the years, honestly sharing some mistakes we had made. Recently, however, I began to answer these questions much more specifically. I made it a point to sit down with many of these new artists and ask them why they felt God was specifically calling them to be a part of the Christian music industry. Many artists give general answers: "well, you know, we really just want to spread the gospel and pray with kids about their lives."

My response: "How?"

The Christian music industry already has enough bands, and especially enough people just making noise. If this is really what God is calling you to do, then how, specifically, is God asking you to make an impact in the lives of people that hear your music?

My intentions are not to destroy the dreams of young musicians; in fact, it's the exact opposite! I really have a desire to see people using their God-given potential to make a difference, and that has to go beyond just playing a guitar. What I'm really trying to get them to explain is how their calling in Christian music equates to carrying a cross. Many bands that we come across will probably sell more records then WILLET, or win awards for their music. All of that is fine as long as God receives the glory. If those album sales and awards are simply lining pockets with a bigger salary and growing self-kingdom, while thousands of children around the world starve to death, then God is not receiving the glory!

In Ezekiel Ch. 33, there are verses that are applicable here:

As for you, son of man, the children of your people are talking about you beside the walls and in the doors of the houses; and they speak to one another, everyone saying to his brother, 'Please come and hear what the word is that comes from the LORD.' So they come to you as people do, they sit before you as My people, and they hear your words, but they do not do them; for with their mouth they show much love, but their hearts pursue their own gain. Indeed you are to them as a very lovely song of one who has a pleasant voice and can play well on an instrument; for they hear your words, but they do not do them. And when this comes to pass—surely it will come—then they will know that a prophet has been among them.[2]

---

[2] Ezekiel 33:30-33

These verses remind us how, within the realm of Christian music, thousands will say to their friends, "come and hear so-and-so play music" or "you just have to hear the music of so-and-so." The question remains though, is it just about the music sounding good? Do people come to a WILLET concert to hear a ***pleasant voice*** or someone who can ***play well on an instrument***?

The president of Food for the Hungry, Ben Homan, commented on WILLET by saying,

"God has granted Jeremy, Justin and Jordan the gift of conveying His heart and passions. When I hear them speak (and sing!), I pause to listen to what the Lord may be saying through them. These are men that I value and trust -- and I count it a joy that Food for the Hungry has the incredible privilege of knowing them and walking alongside their important ministry. They are the real deal."

WILLET exists for the glory of God. We will continue to deny ourselves and carry the cross to the kingdoms of the nations. If WILLET, as a band, or I, personally ever bow down to the cultural suicide of "blending in," it is my prayer that we will be destroyed by the Truth. Somewhere in the world today, a young child is walking to a nearby lake for water. He will take his cup, kneel down, and fill it with water that is being used by the people next to him to wash their clothes and dishes. While in Ethiopia together, we even saw a truck that was backed into the lake and being washed with the same water! Statistically, many people believe that HIV/AIDS causes the most deaths around the world.

They are wrong.

The number one cause of death around the world is unclean water.

Proverbs 31:8-9 says,

Speak up for those who cannot speak for themselves, for the rights of all who are destitute. Speak up and judge fairly; defend the rights of the poor and needy.

In America, we have an abundance to drink. In the past few decades, the clean water coming from our faucets has not been "good enough," so we spend our money on bottled water.

At *Alive Festival* in 2009, I (Jeremy) spent the week speaking on the main stage about orphaned children in Mozambique. I studied some facts about the village of Gorongosa and found this stunning statistic: 25,000 people in the village would share one clean-water well!

25,000 people.

1 clean water well.

Please understand that the water that comes out of that well pails in comparison to the clean water that comes out of your faucet. In an effort to communicate the stat about the well to the 30,000 people at the *Alive Festival*, I walked on stage with one bottle of water as the crowd anticipated the next band (*Switchfoot*). I threw out a few t-shirts, and then asked if anyone could use some water. Thousands of people screamed and put their hands up in an effort to quench their thirst from standing in the sun all day. I explained to them that I would toss the water bottle into the crowd, but it was very important that whoever caught the bottle would share with every person at the festival. As the bottle began to circulate throughout the crowd, we all realized how difficult it really was to share a small amount of water with thousands of people. I continued to explain the great need in Mozambique and offered a way for people to help by sponsoring a child through Food for the Hungry's Child Development Program. As I finished my talk, and the intro music began for *Switchfoot*, the bottle ran out of water after only entering into the hands of approximately 35 people.

Christian author, John Ortberg says,

"A calling, which is something I do for God, is replaced by a career, which threatens to become my god. A career is something I choose for myself; a calling something I receive. A career is something I do for myself; a calling is something I do for God. A career promises status, money or power; a calling generally promises difficulty and even some suffering-and the opportunity to be used by God. A career is about upward mobility' a calling generally leads to downward mobility."[3]

A career is about kingdoms.

A calling is about the cross.

Regarding Ortberg's quote, our dad challenged us with the question of whether WILLET was a calling or a career. In the first three years as a band, each member of our band lived off of a salary of $2,400.00 a year (read that number carefully, not $24,000/year, two-thousand, four hundred dollars and zero cents per year.) In all honesty, you would make more money by working at a fast-food restaurant a few days each week, but we did this on purpose. We didn't accept any other jobs because of our tour schedule, and we just trusted that God would provide along the way.

Career or calling?

As a youth pastor, I (Justin) have taken the students of TBC "engage" youth to dozens of concerts. We have gotten to know many artists and booked bands to play at our events. As Jeremy already mentioned, there are bands that preach and live social justice well. Then, there are bands that teach and preach the Gospel of Jesus Christ well. WILLET has found a balance. Jeremy and his brothers live what they preach and preach what

---

[3] John Ortberg. *If You Want To Walk On Water, You've Got to Get Out of the Boat* (Grand Rapids, MI: Zondervan) p. 71.

they live.

Career or calling?
Our calling to speak on behalf of children around the world who can't speak for themselves has required us to make huge sacrifices in the way we live our lives.

Why?

One word.

Change.

2.25.09
5:34 a.m.
Amsterdam—Journal entry from Jeremy's notebook

Change. You find it in unlikely places. Sometimes in your pocket, other times on your dresser, under the couch, or in the backseat of a car. I recently found change. It was hidden in a small village in eastern Africa called Zeway, Ethiopia.

It is 5:34 a.m. as I purchase a coffee in Amsterdam and await the arrival of our flight back to the U.S. I have just spent seven days in Ethiopia with a team of ten people from Maryland. Two years ago, my brothers (Justin and Jordan) and I traveled to Zeway as a band on a vision trip to learn about the village we were adopting. The children in Ethiopia changed our lives in such a way that we could not stay silent about the poverty we witnessed. Upon returning to the states, we began to promote child sponsorship at every concert and event in which WILLET participated. So far, we have seen over 500 children from Zeway sponsored by people around the country! Praise God! This year, our desire was to get more people involved in the change that is taking place in Ethiopia by leading our first mission trip back to Zeway.

In addition to WILLET, our team consisted of:
- My wife, Kathleen
- Our parents, Glen and Barbara Willet
- Good friend and youth pastor in Maryland, Justin Hanneken
- Our cousins, Jesse and Whitney Willet
- Friend and student from the University of MD, Nicki Brown

Before we even stepped foot on the ground in Ethiopia, I knew that God was with this team. As we worked through the Food for the Hungry (FH) short-term team manual at our preliminary meetings, I began to see the genuine hearts of each team member for the poor. Each of us participated in fundraising for support to cover things like the airfare, in-country costs, and a project that we would be contributing to the community in Zeway. Church members, family and friends from around the country began to show their support by financial contributions or prayer for this trip. Between all ten team members, over $40,000 needed to be raised to cover the cost of the whole trip. We did receive some questions such as,

"Why would you spend $40,000 to help people in Africa while America suffers through an economic crisis?"

Or "Why aren't you helping those in need here in America?"

These questions and more were answered on February 17th, 2009 when we landed in one of the poorest countries in the world. Although we did receive great fundraising support, many team members emptied their savings account to be able to participate in this trip, however, not one team member looked back. Our eyes were attempting to align with God's heart for the poor as we looked ahead to the path that God was leading.

After spending the first night in Addis Ababa, we woke up early on the 18th to meet with Food for the Hungry International (FHI). Twenty-four years ago on that day, I was born in a clean hospital in Westminster, Maryland. Ever since that day, I have had clean water, food, medicine, shelter, education, and a Bible translated in my language. My birthday this year in 2009 would be spent with children and families that have gone without those essential items for most of their lives, and I couldn't think of a better place to be! We spent some time at the FHI office in Addis being briefed about the trip by the Child Development Program director, and our good friend, Feye before driving 3 hours to Zeway. As we traveled the rough roads in two white Range Rovers, we came across over 300 camels! This was a very nice surprise on my birthday as the camel is my favorite animal. We got some great photos but did have to avoid a rock almost being thrown at us by the young boy leading the pack of camels (long story…feel free to ask me sometime). When we arrived in Zeway, we spent some time in orientation with the FH staff at the compound learning about the current status of development taking place in Zeway. Since our last visit, the program has grown from 121 "orphaned and vulnerable children" to over 2046 Orphan and Vulnerable Children (OVC's). One site has expanded to eight sites throughout the surrounding areas, and 42 staff have been deployed to Zeway. After orientation, we spent some time with children on the compound. I later learned this time was being used to set up a surprise celebration for my birthday in the chapel area. Now, before I go on, I need to make it known that it is very difficult for anyone in my family to surprise me with gifts, parties or ideas; however, I did not see this one coming. My wife had emailed the staff prior to our trip, and the team responded with a very special moment. The staff prepared a coffee ceremony, baked a cake, spread popcorn all over the room, sang in Amharic, and presented me with gift of "cultural clothes" complete with a shirt, pants, sandals and a traditional "horse-hair fly swatter". It was a memory that will never be forgotten and I felt humbled to be in the presence of such God-fearing men and women.

In 2007 as a band, we had the opportunity to release a concept project called Virus, which included 10 songs written in Africa, a documentary, 100 photos, and an E-book about the lyrics. On the record was a song we wrote called "For Orphans and the King" (visit www.willetonline.com to listen to the song). The chorus of this song says,

Till the poor will have hope / till the broken find peace
And the hurting will know there is help on the way
Till the hungry are fed / till the children go free
We can't sleep; we are for orphans and The King

As I sat in a small room in Zeway surrounded by social workers, CDP directors, and FH staff, the words of this song came to life. The Bible is full of verses that show that God's heart is with the poor, the lost and the broken, and if we want to experience the fullness of God, we are to live for those people. Sitting in that room, I was humbled to be in the presence of those that have surrendered so much in their own lives for the sake of saving lives!

At the hotel we were staying at in Zeway, there were many days that we would wake up with no running water or electricity. If we are honest, our initial reaction was disappointment and frustration, but as we tried to remain open to what God was teaching us through this trip, we turned each of those moments into opportunities to thank God for what we did have, and remember those that would go without. This was especially true on the day we visited Jiddo. The image that many of us saw that day will never be forgotten. After visiting a small school, we began a few home visits. An hour and a half of rough, dirt road, we came to an area with only a few huts. As we entered this location, we were confronted with crying children, less then six months old, lying in the dirt with no clothes on. Soon, a very frail woman emerged from the hut and sat on a small stool. Through our translator, we learned the haunting reality that this woman only weighed 90 pounds and was seven months pregnant! The pain of sorrow that we experienced in Jiddo was soon replaced with joy as we had the opportunity to visit our sponsored children. Regardless of how many opportunities I have to visit the children that I sponsor, I will never be able to wrap my mind around the beautiful relationship that develops through simple letter writing, photos and prayer. God is in this place.

On this trip, we wanted to contribute more to the community beyond the child sponsorship support that was being provided. During the planning stages of the trip, we learned that the FH compound offices could use a fresh coat of paint. Ironically, our family owned a painting business for years prior to many of us becoming involved in ministry; we put on our painting hats and began to assist the staff. As we prayed a prayer of blessing over the compound, we also painted the words of Micah 6:8, the words, "faith, hope and love" and "God Bless Ethiopia" in both English and Amharic on the office walls. In addition to painting, the team raised over $5000 to build an FH office building in Abossa. We were able to visit this project and also meet some local government officials to say "thank you". The local government had provided this land for free, and joined us in a large circle around the construction in a prayer of blessing. Always trying to keep the children in mind during these projects, some of the money was used to purchase a ping-pong table for the compound so the students had activities to participate in.

During dinner one evening, I had a long conversation with the CDP director, Feye, about the wholistic ministry approach of FH. We discussed social movements such as The ONE Campaign headed by U2 singer, Bono as well as others. Now, for the record, I am a huge U2 fan and very much appreciate the attention that Bono and ONE is bringing to the economic possibilities of fighting poverty. However, along with FH, I strongly agree that the solution to ending extreme poverty goes beyond just finances. Food for the Hungry's approach to care for both the physical and spiritual needs of the poor is one that takes time, but penetrates deep into the community through teamwork and relationship building. I believe that this commitment to the countries that FH is located in will ultimately bring about the change that God intended.

On this trip, each team member had the opportunity to use his or her gifts and talents to serve. Some of us were musicians, and were able to lead worship at team devotions and churches in the area, others were pastors and had the opportunity to preach and lead pastor development sessions, while others were teachers, or nurses, or students or bankers, and were great with children. Each member served with an open heart and spread the joy of the Lord around the village of Zeway.

The word I would use to summarize our return to Zeway this year is: Change. Here are a few specific developments that have taken place in the last two years that I observed:

1. Hospital built by local business owner that operates as a "non-profit" that currently provides affordable treatment and services to patients in need. This hospital employs local health professionals while also partnering with FH's HIV/AIDS awareness program.

2. Over 1700 children sponsored through CDP.

3. Several new hotels and local businesses.

4. Pastor community of over 14 churches in the area working together to spread the love of Jesus.

5. Overall acceptance and understanding of FH's presence in community.

6. Eight FH sites in surrounding areas around Zeway providing relicf assistance.

Change is happening in Zeway. Our prayer is that this will have a ripple effect across the entire country of Ethiopia for the glory of God.

This past Christmas, our family decided that instead of purchasing gifts for each other, we would all put our money together to sponsor a child through Food for the Hungry. During our last day in Zeway, the girl that we had only known through a photo and introductory letter greeted us with a big hug. Genet is a girl that lives in Zeway with her aunt because her parents have died, but has dreams of becoming a professional sports player. As a family, we look forward to seeing Genet's dreams come to life and were honored by the privilege to meet her face to face.

During our debriefing session with the FH staff in Zeway, we found that God was directly in the midst of the plans for this village. Back home in the United States, we had planned a tour called The 500 Faces Tour which would travel all over America in the months following our trip to Africa. The goal of this tour was to see 500 children sponsored before 2010, and would start the week following our return. During the debriefing, we asked the staff if they knew how many additional children needed sponsored. Before the project director, Dawit, even responded, I knew the answer. 500.

On our way back through Addis to the airport, we met up with The Blacksten Family. The Blacksten's are good friends and missionaries that we support through our Dad's church, Quest Community Church. I had the opportunity to ride on the back of his motorbike, weaving in and out of the busy streets of the city on the way to their home. We ate together, prayed and sang some familiar worship songs before shopping at the markets and driving to the airport.

Change is happening in Zeway, and change is happening in my life. God revealed to me some things in my life that I could "go without." Things like my cable television bill...if I would simply cancel my service, I could use that money to sponsor another child (and probably be better off for not watching TV). It's a small sacrifice, but one that will have a lasting impact on a child's life.

On the last day, I wrote some lyrics for a song that I hope to write when I return to the states. It is a collection of thoughts from things that I have experienced this past week in Zeway.[4]

---

[4] To view photos from this trip, please visit www.willetonline.com/photos

kingdoms.

"When poverty and wealth collide, it hits harder then a plane crash and spreads love to the lost and forgotten places. I found God today. He was right where He said he would be. Here In the brokenness. Here In the brokenness."
—WILLET, *from the song "And shout from the rooftop"*

In Galatians 4:4-5, we read these words:

But when the fullness of time had come, God sent forth His Son, born of a woman, born under the law, to redeem those who were under the law, that we might receive the adoption as sons.[1]

The incarnation of Jesus Christ is one place that we find the collision of poverty and wealth. First of all, it happened exactly as God had planned it. Jesus Christ left His throne on high and arrived right on time. He left the praise and adoration of all creation. Creation was made to praise Him. Many times in the Psalms we read phrases such as, **"Praise the LORD from the earth, you great sea creatures and all the depth; Fire and hail, snow and clouds; Stormy wind, fulfilling His word; Mountains and all hills; Fruitful trees and all cedars; Beasts and all cattle; Creeping things and flying fowl."**[2] Not only was Jesus receiving His due praise from creation, He was also receiving praise for thousands of years by those who knew and put their trust in Him. Men and women, children and elderly, have for centuries sang praise, prayed, and declared His testimony. If that's not enough, Revelation 5 gives us a picture of the praise that He received from angels, ten thousand times ten thousand angels.

---

[1] A lot of our friends use language that leads us to believe that they think everyone is born a child of God. Verses like this one and many others lead us to believe otherwise. God is in the business of adoption. No one is born into the family of God, but He allows us to enter in through the blood of His Son. This also leads us to believe that He is a huge fan of adoption as well.

[2] Psalm 148:7-10

God, since the beginning of time, has, and still boasts, an inexhaustible supply of wealth. The scriptures tell us the cattle on a thousand hills are His.[3] There is this phrase that Paul likes to use in the New Testament that speaks of God's wealth:

. . . the riches of His glory . . .

The blessings that God has reserved for His saints are according to the riches of His glory. When Paul says to the Philippian church that his God will supply all their needs, he reminds them that this is done according to the riches of His glory.[4]

This makes sense, does it not? It's not as if God would bless us according to our riches or our glory. We know He won't share His glory with another! In Jeremiah Ch. 9:23, the LORD warns:

**Let not the wise man glory in his wisdom,
Let not the mighty man glory in his might,
Nor let the rich man glory in his riches**

This is what the kingdoms of this world love:

Wisdom.

Might.

Riches.

God wants us to know that even if you have those things, they are not glorious. They are not life-giving or life-sustaining. Instead:

---

[3] Psalm 50:10. Around the time that we were writing this chapter, a dear brother in Christ went home to be with the Lord. His name is Bud Bassler and he owned thousands of cattle throughout his life. Now Bud is at the Throne of Jesus and the cattle are no longer his, which reminds us that they were never actually his to begin with.

[4] Philippians 4:19

*But let him who glories glory in this,
That he understands and knows Me,
That I am the LORD, exercising lovingkindness,
judgment, and righteousness in the earth.
For in these I delight."*[5]

Jesus Christ was born poor. He left His rightful place of glory and exchanged all of that for a humble existence. Shane Claiborne often refers to Jesus as the homeless Rabbi.[6] As He came here, the wealth He always knew collided with the poverty of this world. He exchanged His jealous zeal for our praise (Exodus 34:14), to come and live among us, Emmanuel, God with us. He came not to be served, but to serve and He laid down His crown for a cradle. He gave His life as a ransom for many.[7] Throughout His life, He lived the aforementioned words of Jeremiah 9:24:

Lovingkindness.

Judgment.

Righteousness.

He lived the words of Micah 6:8:

Do Justice.

Love Mercy.

Walk Humbly with God.

In the time of Jeremiah and Micah, our King, Jesus, was exercising these tenets in the world. When He was born among us, Jesus continued the Way of His Kingdom. He

---

[5] Jeremiah 9:24
[6] Claiborne, *The Irresistible Revolution* (Grand Rapids, MI: Zondervan, 2006).
[7] Mark 10:45 and Matthew 20:28

will not change. Jesus is the same, yesterday, today and forever.[8]

When we visited Zeway together in 2009, we did home visits to HIV/AIDS patients with social workers employed by Food for the Hungry. We remember hearing that each social worker cared for over 92 families, and would visit each one at least once a week . . . normally by foot or bicycle. These social workers could easily be making $40,000-$60,000 per year here in the United States; however, they chose to make the sacrifice by living amongst the poor in Ethiopia with a very low salary. Social workers in Zeway, among other Christian social workers around the world, are truly living out the truths found in the Bible. Throughout the Scriptures we can see God's heart for the poor in verses such as:

If there is a poor man among your brothers in any of the towns of the land that the LORD your God is giving you, do not be hardhearted or tightfisted toward your poor brother. Rather be openhanded and freely lend him whatever he needs. Be careful not to harbor this wicked thought: "The seventh year, the year for canceling debts, is near," so that you do not show ill will toward your needy brother and give him nothing. He may then appeal to the LORD against you, and you will be found guilty of sin. Give generously to him and do so without a grudging heart; then because of this the LORD your God will bless you in all your work and in everything you put your hand to. There will always be poor people in the land. Therefore I command you to be openhanded toward your brothers and toward the poor and needy in your land.[9]

He who oppresses the poor shows contempt for their Maker, but whoever is kind to the needy honors God.[10]

---

[8] Hebrews 13:8, see also Malachi 3:6
[9] Deuteronomy 15:7-11
[10] Proverbs 14:31

Speak up for those who cannot speak for themselves, for the rights of all who are destitute. Speak up and judge fairly; defend the rights of the poor and needy.[11]

Share with God's people who are in need. Practice hospitality.[12]

After holding the hands of the poor, it's impossible for us not to speak on their behalf. As God has granted us this privilege, we have experienced some unusual side effects. Waking up in the middle of the night, haunted by the statistics that we use when we speak on behalf of the beautiful children of Zeway is quite common. In addition, we ourselves have wrestled with our wealth in comparison to those we have met in the nations. Should we subscribe to cable service? Should we even own a TV?

The following statistics are from www.fh.org:

•Every day 25,000 people die from hunger and hunger-related causes? Of those, 18,000 are children. One person dies of hunger every 3.6 seconds. That is more than 17 people each minute; 1,042 each hour; which translates into 9,125,000 every single year!

•One in six people on the planet is hungry.

•In the last 50 years, more than 418 million people have died from hunger and poor sanitation--nearly three times the number of people who died in all wars of the 20th century.

•The real reason nearly one billion of the planet's 6.7 billion people are undernourished is because of food-distribution problems, natural disasters, government policies, civil unrest, inequitable trade policies, lack of knowledge and greed.

---

[11] Proverbs 31:8-9
[12] Romans 12:13

- 33.2 million people have HIV/AIDS, including 2.1 million children and 19 million women.

- 2.5 million new HIV infections every year, including 420,000 children

- 2.1 million AIDS-related deaths annually

Rob Bell reminds us in his RICH NOOMA video, 92% of people in the world do not own a car. That makes us part of the richest 8% of the world's population. Something is terribly wrong.

As lovers of the Heavenly Kingdom, it's easy for us to assume that other lovers of His Kingdom would get on board with this quickly. That's simply not the case. In a recent Barna Research poll, the study yielded this dagger of a statistic: 2% of evangelical Christians said they would give financially to a "Christian Organization ministering to an AIDS orphan" in Africa.[13]

"Our generation will be remembered by three things: the Internet, the war on terror, and how we let an entire continent go up in flames while we stood around with watering cans..."[14]—Bono

98% of the wealthy will not help their impoverished brethren.
98% of evangelical Christians hold watering cans.

Not only did poverty and wealth collide at the birth of Jesus, kingdoms collided as well.

When we say in the subtitle of this book that the world is in love with kingdoms, we are referring to materialism,

---

[13] Jenny Eaton and Kate Etue. *The aWAKE Project: UNITING AGAINST THE AFRICAN AIDS CRISIS* (Nashville, Tennessee, W. Publishing Group, 2002).

[14] Steve Stockman. *Walk On: The Spiritual Journey of U2* (Orlando: Relevant Books, 2005), p. 205.

consumerism, and patriotism. Deep inside every one of us, there seems to be a longing to be a part of something. In America, from an early age we are taught to pledge allegiance to the kingdom of America. In our teenage years, we pledge allegiance to the kingdoms, cliques and societies that best suit our desire to belong. In college, we rebel and form our own kingdoms.

Kingdoms are quite tempting. At their core, they promise power, and power is tempting. Is it any wonder that when Jesus went into the wilderness with the devil, he tempted Him with power and kingdoms?

Again, the devil took Him up on an exceedingly high mountain, and showed Him all the kingdoms of the world and their glory. [15]

Satan offers the Son of God the sub-par kingdoms of the world in exchange for worship. Amazing. How much does worship play a part in our allegiance to kingdoms? Perhaps more than anything else!

We live in an interesting time in history. The most successful artists in the Christian music scene have their songs categorized in the style of worship. Not to mention, social justice is "in-style."

We say it is an "interesting time in history" because both worship and social justice should never be "in-style." If we are living as the scriptures command us to, both of these ideals should not make us popular, but rather should get us killed!

In the Christian community, worship has been diluted to a style within Contemporary Christian music. The artists that play this "style" have #1 singles on the radio, Grammy nominations for the #1 selling albums, and sold-out tours around the world. Why is this so? Because we associate worship as a style of music and an experience at an event rather then a lifestyle surren-

---

[15] Matthew 4:8

dered to the King! As we thirst for that next experience, we slowly begin to build up our kingdom of materialism by purchasing music, concert tickets and books about worship in an effort to draw near to our Savior. Now, don't get us wrong . . . there is definitely a place for songs of praise to be written and sung to our God within the church. However, there is also an equally important place for us to live a life of worship and be the Church. In fact, the most important aspect about "church" is not when you walk through the doors, but rather what you do when you walk back out.

Remember the social workers in Zeway that we shared about? There is one in particular that we had the opportunity to meet. Her name was Tigist Shibre. Tigist truly lived out social justice. She didn't buy a trendy t-shirt with an Africa logo on it. She didn't write her email on a sign-up form and wear a cute white bracelet. She didn't even lobby her congressman about sending money to fight aids.

She lived amongst the poor.

On June 9th, 2009, Tigist died amongst the poor as well.[16]

Social justice didn't make her popular or win her awards. It killed her in an accident on the way to serve "the least of these." Tigist ignored the pressure of building her earthly kingdom in exchange for a simple life amongst the poor. You would have never heard of her on this earth, had we not told you her story. We need more people like Tigist because time is most definitely running out. God is calling His children to step outside cultural boundaries and live a life of freedom and responsibility to be the hands and feet of Christ.

But what does this look like? What does God require of us as we go through life here on earth?

---

[16] This book is dedicated to Tigist and the children that she ministered to.

As we begin our discussion of kingdoms, we feel the need to remind you, and ourselves, that every kingdom will fail.

Except one.

If you join the Unfailing Kingdom and align your life to the practices of its King, 1 Peter 1:4 speaks of your reward:

An incorruptible inheritance, undefiled that does not fade away, reserved for you in heaven . . .

Again, God can give this inheritance because He is rich! But the truth is that most people are not interested in the Unfailing Kingdom. They want to build their own kingdoms, complete with wisdom, might, riches and ocean front property. Jesus said the Way to His Kingdom is narrow. It is much easier and more appealing to walk where everyone else is walking, the path of the world's kingdoms, then to follow after Him.

In 2009, there were three major celebrities that died over the course of one week. Television stations scheduled to air remembrance stories on the first two deaths were interrupted by the sudden death of the 'king of pop.' Within hours, fans gathered around the hospital to hold vigils throughout the night, as thousands of others gathered in major cities around the world to remember the star. Social networking sites watched as millions updated their status to voice their opinions of his death, and it was reported that the Internet actually slowed down on this day due to heavy traffic of people searching for articles on the story. At the time of his death, it was reported that his income was approximately 19 million dollars a year; however, only days after his death, many of his possessions, his estate and belongings were sold. Why is this significant?

The king of pop is dead.

The king of pop is not coming back.

His name won't actually be mentioned in this book to prove a point, yet millions of people made him an important part of their lives.

The kingdom that he built here on earth was sold within days of his passing.

Kingdoms not built in Heaven will pass away. Check out: Matthew 6:19-20.

We love the confession of a man, King Hezekiah in 2 Kings 19,

"O LORD God of Israel, the One who dwells between the cherubim, You are God, You alone, of all the kingdoms of the earth. You have made heaven and earth."

People who head up the many kingdoms of this earth believe that they own those kingdoms. They believe that they built, maintained and sustained them. As Hezekiah's prayer continues, four verses later he declares,

Now therefore, O LORD our God, I pray, save us from his hand, that all the kingdoms of the earth may know that You are the LORD God, You alone."[17]

When earthly kingdoms ask God for help, such as America in the weeks following September 11, 2001, they are asking a God, whom they neither know nor acknowledge, to intervene on their behalf. This is relative deism. When Hezekiah and Isaiah asked God for help, they took a different approach: declaring that God's help would let ***"all the kingdoms on the earth"*** know who the true King is. They were interested in God's fame. This reminds us of a verse:

Yes, Lord, walking in the way of Your truth,
O Lord, we have waited for You,

---

[17] See also the similar words of Isaiah (contemporary of Hezekiah) in Isaiah 37:20.

The desire of our souls is Your Name and Your renown,
And for the remembrance of You. [18]

Soon, and very soon, all of the kingdoms of the world will belong to their rightful owner, the King Jesus! Revelation 11:15 will come to pass. Isn't it just like our God to take ownership over something incredibly despicable and change it, mold it, and become Lord of it?

If you are not part of the Kingdom that is coming, but rather pledge your allegiance to a kingdom that is yours, or governed by someone you don't know, you may want to spend some time looking at Psalm 79:6. We'd include it here for you, but we really would rather you read it for yourself.

If by chance you are saying, "Guys, I'm already on board with the Heavenly Kingdom, I really love it!" we are excited for you. We also want to make sure that you are not just in love with it, but dying for it as well.

---

[18] Isaiah 26:8 NKJV blended with NASB

salt.

We have sought to establish and support several notions in this text. First, there are people who think they are carrying the cross like Jesus, and there are people that are actually carrying crosses.[1] Second, we have divulged into the narcissistic tendency of man towards kingdom-building and all that selfishness and materialism represents. We could easily stop there and challenge you to go the opposite way, but we sense there is a third group that we have yet to represent in this quest. There are those who are so in love with the heavenly Kingdom of Jesus that their actions here on earth do not reflect the heart of their very Savior. In James 2:17, the Scriptures tell us, **"faith by itself, if it does not have works, is dead."** The pursuit of an eternity with Jesus (the Heavenly Kingdom) is through faith, but should be supported through actions (while amongst the world's kingdoms). This reminds us of the notion that God wants us to be in the world, not of the world.[2]

"It's been said that you can't be so heavenly minded that you are of no earthly good. I'd like to present to some and introduce to others the Lord Jesus the Christ: the epitome of being heavenly minded and of earthly good."
—*Cross Movement, from the song, "Who's the Man?"*

Your attitude should be the same as that of Christ Jesus: Who, being in very nature God, did not consider equality with God something to be grasped, but made Himself nothing, taking the very nature of a servant, being made in human likeness. And being found in appearance as a man, He humbled Himself

---

[1] Regarding regulations and the doctrines of men, *Colossians 2:23 says,* **"These things indeed have an appearance of wisdom in self-imposed religion, false humility, and neglect of the body, but are of no value against the indulgence of the flesh."** In other words, the same things can be said of someone that thinks he is carrying the cross, but have in fact been carrying something else, something self-imposed, something of no Kingdom value.

[2] See also: Colossians 2:8, John 17:14, Romans 12:2, James 1:27b, 1 John 2:15.

and became obedient to death- even death on a cross! [3]

Jesus was in love with His Father's Kingdom so much that He provided the perfect example to us of how we should love His Kingdom.

Serve others.

When I (Jeremy) was growing up, we would hold many family gatherings at my grandparents' house. My great-aunt lived next door and I remember looking across the bushes and seeing her sitting in the window reading her Bible and praying, wondering if she ever left her house. She was a quiet, frail lady, but was deeply in love with God. When my great-aunt Margaret passed away, the pastor read a note that she wrote and requested to be read to the congregation. The note said,

"Remember to give God all the glory."

Following the funeral, I thought a lot about the life of my great-aunt. I contemplated if the reason she spent so much time praying and reading the scriptures was because she was so in love with the Kingdom of Jesus that she was simply waiting for her time to go home.

I was wrong.

In the last few years of her life, she was unable to drive and had to rely on other people to provide transportation. This would explain why we saw her inside her house so much. I later learned that she spent this time reading the Bible, praying, and writing letters of encouragement to missionaries.[4] We would often see large campers parked in her driveway, and found out that she opened her home and hospitality to traveling missionaries when they came through Maryland.[5] She didn't have a lot, and wasn't able to travel to many of the places that

---

[3] Philippians 2:5-8
[4] 1 Thessalonians 5:17
[5] Genesis 19:2a

she prayed for, but she was being used by God in a mighty way!

My great-aunt Margaret was in love with Jesus and His Kingdom.

By reading the Scriptures, she knew what it meant to be in love with the Kingdom of Jesus.

She served others.

In 2008, my wife and I (Jeremy) bought our first home.

It belonged to my great-aunt Margaret.

I wrote this chapter in the room where she sat and prayed:

Every.

Single.

Day.

I now sit in that room and pray for a missionary in Haiti.

My wife.

I (Justin) told you about my dad back in Chapter 3. His name is Gary but he'd much rather you not know his name. Jesus Christ radically rescued him on June 23rd of 1999. Dad realized that for the first 41 years of his life, he took all the glory for himself. He was good at just about everything he tried and was quick to tell you about it—that is, until Jesus Christ saved dad.

To God be the Glory: this became Dad's new motto for his life. Perhaps you are familiar with the phrase, or sang the hymn in church, but dad lives it, literally. Within a few months of his rescue, dad created a shirt with that saying printed very large on the back. On the front, it said "Jesus."

For the past 10 years, dad has worn the same shirt:

Every.

Single.

Day.

At first they were just printed in purple, now they have been printed in dozens of colors. Even when attending an "important" event, he'll still wear the Jesus shirt under his suit jacket. Not only does dad wear the witness tee every day, but he has given away thousands of them. His car is wrapped in Scripture and JESUS and he walks with a shofar[6] on his arm. Dad cannot go anywhere without carrying the cross with him, to God be the glory!

***Jesus did many other things as well. If every one of them were written down, I suppose that even the whole world would not have room for the books that would be written.*[7]**

The Bible shows us that Jesus served as a Man walking the earth. The stories included in Scripture are only a portion of the ways He helped other people because many of them were never recorded! As Christians called to be Christ-like, we need to continue the example set by our Savior. If you have been a Christian for more than five minutes, we sense that you have heard this beautiful saying of Jesus in the Sermon on the Mount:

***You are the salt of the earth; but if the salt loses its flavor, how shall it be seasoned? It is then good for nothing but to be thrown out and trampled underfoot by men.*[8]**

---

[6] A shofar is a ram's horn that was used in Biblical times to signify a battle or sound of worship to God.
[7] John 21:25
[8] Matthew 5:13

For a long time, we have wondered what Jesus actually means when He calls us salt?

Nearly 2,000 years have passed since this saying was first spoken, and recorded. We find ourselves in a time period where people love to argue that the Bible is not literal. We believe the words of the Bible to mean the same thing when they were written as they do now. So, naturally, we think of salt as adding flavor to things. Have you ever tried fresh-cut french fries without salt? It's nothing to get excited about. So, because salt is used for flavor, we assume that Jesus wants us to be His flavor to the earth.

Makes sense, doesn't it? The verse quoted above comes from the Gospel of Matthew. This is the first mention in the New Testament of the word salt. It also appears in the Gospels of Mark and Luke.

Mark quotes Jesus as He says: ***For everyone will be seasoned with fire, and every sacrifice will be seasoned with salt. Salt is good, but if salt loses its flavor, how will you season it? Have salt in yourselves, and have peace with one another.***[9]

After reading Jesus' thoughts as recorded by Mark on salt, we see that these two verses support our notion that Jesus doesn't want us to lose flavor. In addition, we find out that a practical manner for not losing flavor is forgiveness, or peace with one another.

Next, let's see what Luke has to say about salt:

"Salt is good; but if the salt has lost its flavor, how shall it be seasoned? It is neither fit for the land nor for the dunghill, but men throw it out. He who has ears to hear, let him hear!"[10]

---

[9] Mark 9:49-50
[10] Luke 14:34-35

Luke records the words of Jesus regarding salt as well, and this immediately follows verses that speak about being His disciple. So, if Jesus wants His followers to be salty, we have to find out what He means by this, or else, we are not even fit for the land nor for the dunghill.[11]

Before we reveal what we sense Jesus is saying here in these verses, check out what Paul says to the church at Colossae:

Let your speech always be with grace, seasoned with salt, that you may know how you ought to answer each one [outsiders to the faith]. [12]

So, we can glean from what the Spirit said through Paul, that the manner in which we speak to people, if filled with grace, we are in fact bringing salt to the unbelievers.

What were some foods that were eaten by people in the 1st century? We know from the Gospels that people ate fish. In addition, from several places in the New Testament, we know that people ate meat.

Fish and meat.

In the first century, there were no refrigerators (we didn't see any in Ethiopia in 2009 either). According to the US Food and Drug Administration, all foods (not just fish and meat) that have been left out for more than 2 hours between 40 and 140 degrees Fahrenheit should be discarded.[13] Pathogenic bacteria on food will not "generally affect the taste, smell, or appearance of a food" but will double every twenty minutes.

So, how is food preserved? Well, you have 2 choices: change its temperature or use salt.

---

[11] manure!
[12] Colossians 4:6
[13] www.fda.gov

Salt.

Not just for flavor, but for preserving the life of food.

If salt preserves the life of food and Jesus calls us to be salt, is it possible that we are preserving the life of the earth?
pre-serve [pri-zurv]—to keep alive or in existence; make lasting[14]

The earth is going to die. Some day it's going to cease to exist. God is going to destroy and re-create it.[15] If this saddens you, we highly recommend that you put your faith and trust in Jesus Christ.

The good news is that God is not going to destroy the earth while His remnant is still in it. The very presence of true Christians, bearers of the cross, in the world, represents His Light still shining. Things will not always be this way.

Jeremiah 7:34 speaks of some events that occurred historically and will occur again prophetically:

Then I will cause to cease from the cities of Judah and from the streets of Jerusalem the voice of mirth and the voice of gladness, the voice of the bridegroom and the voice of the bride. For the land shall be desolate.

Mirth.

Mirth is another word for joy. There will be no joy left on the earth once God's rapture occurs.[16]

Gladness.

---

[14] www.dictionary.com

[15] 2 Peter 3:13, Is. 65:17, Is. 66:22a, Revelation 21:1

[16] Before you let us know that the word "rapture" does not appear in Scripture, we want you to know that we realize that. We do however believe that this mysterious event is true and will in fact happen, despite what some of our friends think.

Gladness will cease on the earth. What will the people have to be glad about? The Salt of the earth and the Light of the world will be taken out of the world. If you think the earth is a dark place in 2009 (so do we), you can't even imagine how dark it will be in the end of days.

Bridegroom.

The Bridegroom will not speak. If you are not sure who is meant by Bridegroom, check out Joel 2:16, Matthew 9:15. The Bridegroom is in fact our King, Jesus. For centuries, God has spoken on the earth. He has spoken audibly to men, and He has spoken through His prophets. One day, He will be silent.

The Bride.

In the Scriptures, Jesus' Church is often referred to as His bride. It would make sense, seeing as He is the Bridegroom. As we pick up crosses and follow Him, we are adorning ourselves as a wife for her husband.[17]

When the end of days comes to pass, the Bride will no longer be on the earth because Jesus Christ Himself will take us to be with Him. We could write for hours on the Rapture, but we'd much rather you read about it for yourself in 1 Thessalonians 4.

The end of Jeremiah 7:34 says that the land shall be desolate. Some day, hopefully soon, Jesus Christ is going to destroy this earth and introduce His bride to the New Heaven and New Earth, but as we stated before, He will not do this while we, His people, are still on the earth.

How do you feel when you think of God as a Destroyer? When we introduce Him as a Destroyer, do any cities or countries come to mind?

---

[17] John 3:29, Revelation 21:2, Revelation 21:9, Revelation 22:17

When I (Justin) asked these questions to the students of TBC "engage" Youth, they responded enthusiastically, "Sodom and Gomorrah!" I said, "Exactly!"

Sodom and Gomorrah.

In Genesis, Abraham intercedes for one of these cities. His nephew Lot was dwelling in Sodom, so Abraham talks to God and bargains for the existence of that city. He says to God:

"Would You also destroy the righteous with the wicked? Suppose there were fifty righteous within the city; would You also destroy the place and not spare it for the fifty righteous that were in it? Far be it from You to do such a thing as this, to slay the righteous with the wicked, so that the righteous should be as the wicked; far be it from You! Shall not the Judge of all the earth do right?" So the LORD said, "If I find in Sodom fifty righteous within the city, then I will spare all the place for their sakes."[18]

The bargaining begins. Abraham approaches God and bargains from fifty righteous down to ten. Is God going to find ten righteous in Sodom and not destroy it? No way! God sends some angelic messengers to visit Lot. Lot is speaking with the visitors in the doorway of his house and the sick, twisted, and wicked of the city come to attempt to know...carnally[19] the angelic visitors.

Then the men said to Lot, "Have you anyone else here? Son-in-law, your sons, your daughters, and whomever you have in the city—take them out of this place! For we will destroy this place, because the outcry against them has grown great before the face of the LORD, and the LORD has sent us to destroy it."[20]

---

[18] Genesis 18:23-26
[19] Genesis 19:5
[20] Genesis 19:12-13

God sent His angelic visitors to destroy the city. They did not need to search for 10 righteous. God is omniscient, and He knew there were no righteous there. Nevertheless, He chose to rescue Lot and his family.

Why did God destroy these two cities? Genesis 19 says because of the outcry against them. In Sunday school, we have been taught and have been teaching for years that Sodom and Gomorrah were destroyed because of the sin of homosexuality. We know this is true, but it's not the only reason.

Look, this was the iniquity of your sister Sodom: She and her daughter had pride, fullness of food, and abundance of idleness; neither did she strengthen the hand of the poor and needy. And they were haughty and committed abomination before Me; therefore I took them away as I saw fit. [21]

Homosexuality.

Pride.

Fullness of food.

Abundance of idleness.

Neglect of the poor and needy.

Haughty.

Do these traits sound familiar to you? God sees fit to destroy Sodom and Gomorrah, but He does not do so until He warns Lot and gives him time to get his family out of the city. Once the people of God are gone, the destruction can begin.

As Lot and his family lingered, the angels interceded and brought them out of the city safely. One angel turns to

---

[21] Ezekiel 16:49-50

them and gives the following instruction: ***"Do not look behind you!"***[22]

Lot's wife is disobedient. She looks back and becomes: A Pillar of:

Salt.

Eventually trampled underfoot by men.[23]

God is preserving us. 1 Thessalonians 5:23 tells us that He is making us blameless at His coming. Luke 17:33 indicates that when we carry the cross of Jesus Christ and live for His Kingdom, in the loss of our life, we are actually winning because He is involved.

God is preserving us.

We are, in turn, preserving the earth.

Every.

Single.

Day.

But what does that even look like?

---

[22] Genesis 19:17
[23] Matthew 5:13

water.

> **Breakfast**
> **+ Lunch**
> **+ Snack**
> **+ Dinner**
> **+ Bedtime snack =**
> **Average American Daily Diet**

A girl in Pennsylvania recently decided that this diet was too much when she learned that 30,000 people around the world would die today from starvation. In chapter 6, we printed a quote by Bono that said,

"Our generation will be remembered by three things: the Internet, the war on terror, and how we let an entire continent go up in flames while we stood around with watering cans . . ."

We left off two words:

"Or not."

We don't know about you, but we do not want our generation to be remembered for that last item. We find it interesting that Bono uses the words "watering cans" when referencing the fire in Africa. When we think of a blazing fire, we normally attribute the solution to fire departments arriving with trucks, ladders, helicopters carrying water, and rescue equipment. Bono didn't mention an emergency squad. He used the words, "watering cans." Whether or not Bono was intentionally emphasizing this illustration, his statement carries a very valuable lesson in the fight against extreme poverty.

I (Jeremy) was speaking at a school in Pennsylvania during WILLET's Virus Tour.[1] I spent a lot of time talking about our recent trips to Africa, showing videos from these trips, and explaining how each student can be a

---

[1] www.willetonline.com/virustour

part of change happening around the world. Through our partnership with Food for the Hungry, we always offer the opportunity to sponsor an orphaned child for $32/month. Following the assembly, a girl named Amanda approached me and said that she wanted to help one of the orphaned children. She went on to explain; however, that she had no source of income. No job, no allowance, and no savings. As she shared this with me, I said,

"I understand. Maybe you would be willing to at least pray for them?"

She quickly stopped me and said,

"Well, I will definitely pray for them, but I would like to actually sponsor a child."

I thought to myself, "How is this going to be possible with no money?"

"You see, everyday for lunch, my parents give me $2.15 to buy school lunch." Amanda said. "While you were talking on stage, I realized that everyday I wake up I have clean clothes to put on, breakfast, lunch, a snack, dinner and another snack before I go to bed. That is too much when a child is dying for the lack of clean water! If I saved up my lunch money, I would have enough each month to sponsor a child!"

That day in Pennsylvania, Amanda sponsored an 8-year-old boy from Ethiopia.

Amanda is 11-years-old.

Amanda does not eat lunch anymore.

An orphan in Africa eats.

> **Breakfast**
> **+ Lunch**
> **+ Snack**
> **+ Dinner**
> **+ Bedtime snack**
> **- Lunch =** _____
>   **Progress**

"If you can't feed a hundred people, then feed just one."
—Mother Teresa

There is a fire raging around the world. According to The World Bank, there are more then 1 billion people living on less then $1 per day. There are Americans whose personal wealth is above the wealth of several countries combined. Children in Haiti make their beds on a slab of cardboard in the middle of the street while orphans in Ethiopia die from HIV. A girl in India is sold into prostitution while a Christian church is burned to the ground in Rwanda. Thousands are forced to work in sweatshops in Cambodia for cents a day while a 6-year-old boy is handed an AK-47 in Uganda.
Are you ready to carry that watering can yet?

Better yet, are you ready to carry the cross?

At Purple Door 2009, speaker Eric Samuel Timm talked about some of the same atrocities. He said, "Among the broken, don't ask "God, where are you?" rather ask, "God, where are Your people?" If more Christians took Jesus' command to carry the cross seriously, the question would not even have to be asked.

Back in Chapter 2, Jeremy wrote about living the Christian life, and ministering to young people. God later showed him that those things did not equate to carrying the cross. I (Justin) have had similar revelations throughout my walk with Christ. Just because I have a youth ministry that Christians call 'successful,' and just because I have the privilege of writing and relaying messages from the Holy Spirit to teenagers 52 weeks a year, does not automatically equate to carrying the cross.

When a group of skaters go to Baltimore to skate Charm City and minister to the homeless at the same time, a cross is carried.

When 18 teenagers from TBC "engage" youth show up to a week-long Vacation Bible School simply to love, serve and minister to children, a cross is carried.

When the phone rings at 1am, and a door is opened, a conversation takes place, and prayers are lifted, a cross is carried.

When dozens of students, year after year go without food for 30 (sometimes 48-60) hours so that others around the world can eat, a cross is carried.

When high-school seniors spend their spring break, or summer vacation on mission trips rather than the alternative, a cross is carried.

Recently, God showed us a two-year-old who carried a cross. In June 2009, I (Justin) took my family on vacation to the Outer Banks. On the drive home, we were heading up 95-North. My wife drove as I listened to music and wrote a chapter for this very book. All of a sudden, the phone rang from an unknown caller. I answered.

The caller was a girl who came through our youth group years ago, trusted Christ (on Christmas Day!) and later went her own way. She met a guy and she eventually gave birth to a little girl who, at the time of the call, was seven months old. The baby's name is Sade. They moved around, ended up in Texas for a while and, last I had heard, she was living there. After a quick greeting, she said, "I've got a surprise for you, I'm in Baltimore!" I was startled by this, but later found out that she had left the guy because he was abusing her. She called the police, they arrested him, and her grandparents sent her a one-way plane ticket back to Maryland.

As she went to the airport in Houston with four full suitcases, she had no money, so they wouldn't let her take the suitcases on the plane. Here she was, in Baltimore, with 7-month-old-Sade, and very few possessions. God brought this girl into our life a long time ago, and here she was again. We bear a cross for her. We always have, and we always will. After speaking with her, I immediately called another one of our cross-bearing youth leaders. She called another cross-bearing woman, and a large quantity of gently used baby stuff was collected for Sade over-night. Fortunately, we have two baby girls so we were able to contribute a lot of their out-grown clothes. We went to church that morning and afterwards we went to go and visit her. We stopped at a store and bought her the biggest box of diapers they had. We arrived at her house and she was overjoyed at the amount of gifts. We took her out to lunch and heard her stories. We prayed for her and Sade and God ushered us into picking up the cross for Sade. As we were saying goodbye to her, her grandmother came out of the house. She came up to me, hugged me and said, "We scrounged up every dollar we had to get her a plane ticket to bring her here. I felt bad because I knew we wouldn't have any money to get stuff for the baby. I just kept praying and asking God to provide and He did through you."

He.

Did.

To God be the glory! We got in the car and could not speak. As we drove up the highway, the voice of our two-year-old daughter, Gloria, resounded from the backseat:

"Mommy, I think Sade want go to Jesus house with me."

All we could do was cry. Is it possible that at two-years-old, Gloria picked up a cross for her new friend?

Assuredly, I say to you, whoever does not receive the kingdom of God as a little child will by no means enter it.[2]

Gloria carries a cross for Sade, and the three children we sponsor as well. Her prayers to God are so precious and they almost always include these four children's names (without our prompting).

You are never too young or too old to carry the cross and it is our desire that once you pick up a cross, you would not set it back down. Rather, you would cling to it, love it, cherish it and die with it. This is more God's desire than it is ours. Do you remember what differentiated the same saying in Mark 8:34 from Luke 9:23? It was one word: Daily.

As we mentioned earlier, fires burn daily. The AIDS fire in Africa has been burning for over twenty-five years straight.

25 years.

Deadly fire.

Daily.

It is time to stop relying on the US government to put out the fire.[3] The rescue squad that politicians have been promising (and failing to deliver for years) must be replaced by a generation willing to carry the cross on their backs while holding the Living Water in both hands. When our individual efforts come together, we become stronger, and that's when children around the world receive help. There is no one person that can end extreme poverty.

We believe in a God that can.

---

[2] Mark 10:15

[3] We are thankful however for an USAID Grant that provided for this book. As the front cover states, your book purchase sends $20 in Aid to the nations! Praise God.

Author Mark Batterson calls this: living life with "a fundamental conviction: God is able."[4]

Throughout this entire book, we have presented a discussion on kingdoms and carrying the cross.[5] In the Bible, we find only one passage in Scripture where the words carried and kingdom both appear.

"You yourselves have seen what I [God] did to Egypt, and how I carried you on eagles' wings and brought you to Myself. Now if you obey Me fully and keep My covenant, then out of all nations you will be My treasured possession. Although the whole earth is mine, you will be for me a kingdom of priests and a holy nation."[6]

When you see the words "eagles' wings" in this verse, perhaps you think of the often-quoted Isaiah 40:31:

But those who wait on the LORD shall renew their strength; They shall mount up with wings like eagles, They shall run and not be weary, They shall walk and not faint.

As often as we hear people quote this verse, we rarely hear anyone explain what it means for us to soar on wings like eagles. Sure, it sounds nice in a Christian song, but what does it really refer to? This phrase is a reference to the Exodus. To soar on wings like eagles is an expression that exemplifies the God of Scripture carrying His people out of slavery and into the Promised Land. For us to be carried on eagles' wings is to be lifted by God, from a life intent on living for the kingdoms of this world, to a life spent carrying the cross of the Holy Kingdom.

---

[4] Mark Batterson. Wild Goose Chase. (Colorado Springs: Mulnomah Press, 2008), p. 85.
[5] See p. 132.
[6] Exodus 19:4-6a, underlines added

Notice as well, in this verse, the words: **obey me fully, keep my covenant.** God challenges us to obey His covenant so that we become people of His Kingdom. The Bible is very clear on how we are to obey His covenant (remember our study on garments?) and He calls us His kingdom of priests and His holy nation.[7]

We don't need more money, power, people, or even more churches to fight extreme poverty.

We need the Church to be the kingdom of priests.

We need the Church to be the holy nation.

We need Jesus Christ manifested through our lives.

Daily.

In our lives, we found that once we walked outside of the church, we got a glimpse of the hurting world around us. It broke our hearts. We couldn't ignore the brokenness because God is in the brokenness. Although there are many options and organizations to consider when you attempt to serve the least of these, we are firm believers in a unique avenue called, child sponsorship. What started as one child sponsored from one village in Ethiopia in 2007, has now grown to over one thousand children (and counting) in three different villages adopted through WILLET. We strongly endorse the holistic ministry approach of organizations like Food for the Hungry. FH cares for the physical and spiritual needs of children around the world by providing food, clean water, medicine, clothing and education, but also by supplying children with Bibles translated into their own languages. In addition, we are also passionate about relief and development taking place in a community as we have witnessed the impact of this first hand. (If we ever get a chance to meet each other, ask us about what we

---

[7] In the back of this book, we have included a short group study for you to complete after reading *carried*. This study provides scripture references on how we are to serve the poor, as well as a scripture study on the word *carried* on p. 132.

saw in a place called Jiddo.) After a natural disaster, conflict, famine or drought, relief is needed as soon as possible. However, the next step (and most important step in our opinion) is to come alongside a community for development. During the relief stage, essential items are simply being supplied. The development stage however shows the people how to provide for themselves to break the devastating cycle of poverty. Coupled with this, child sponsorship offers a very unique form of assistance through relationship building. When you sponsor a child through FH, you are the only sponsor of that particular child, and you can begin writing letters and sharing photos of you and your family!

In February of 2009, I (Justin) joined the WILLET team on a trip to Ethiopia. It was on this trip that I experienced one of the most amazing moments of my life: I got to meet my FH sponsor-child.

Goytom is 10 years old. His dad died three years ago, and he lives with his mom, and five siblings, in a house the size of my living room. As we drove down his street, his social worker pointed him out in the distance. He was approaching his house carrying a load of wood. This is significant because it is a direct reflection of who Goytom is. He is a hard worker. He carries wood, like Isaac, and carries water like the woman at the well in John 4. Goytom is a hard worker.

As I got to know Goytom, we spoke through a translator. He smiled the entire time and I cried tears of joy. As we went from the courtyard into Goytom's house, he had something to show me. It was the letters I had written him. The one in particular he handed me was very special. I wrote it just three weeks prior to that very Zeway trip. In that letter, it said: "I hope to come and visit you some day." At that moment, the weight of the situation hit me.

Goytom held a letter that I had written him, and in just three weeks, he had it, translated in his language, delivered to his house, by the same man who translated our conversations and also translated Goytom's letters back to me.

> **FOOD FOR THE HUNGRY INTERNATIONAL/ ETHIOPIA-Zeway Project**
> **Response Letter for sponsors**
>
> [Amharic handwritten text]
>
> Child's signature: [signature]
>
> Child Name: Goytom Akez Tsause
> Child ID: 188-011-1205
> Sponsor Name: Hanneken, Justin
>
> Dear Hanneken Justin, how are you? Your family? My family and I am fine. Thank you for your letter. God bless you. Now I have one week to join my school. Because there was mid-semester rest. Through this time I spent by helping my family at home and by studying. I like playing foot ball. God bless you all when you are doing.
>
> Sincerely,
> Goytom Akete
>
> Translator Name: Soloman Zeleke   signature: [signature]

In that moment, something that I always believed was real became an absolute reality.

After getting home from Ethiopia, I had to share what I had seen and experienced. I told Goytom's story over and over, to anyone I could, as often as possible. Before leaving for Ethiopia, WILLET as a band pledged to God that they would, by His great grace, get 500 kids from Zeway sponsored by 2010. Before we left in February, the total was six kids. It is now July 2009, and more than 310 kids have been sponsored.

Not only does this opportunity affect the child you are sponsoring, God uses child sponsorship to revolutionize lives here in the US. See page 113 for an article in 6:8 Magazine from a road journal that WILLET submitted from a prior tour.

God continues to use an independent band with no record label support to impact the lives of thousands around the world.

God continues to use a youth pastor with a limited budget to impact the lives of thousands around the world.

God will use *you* to impact the lives of thousands around the world.

What does it mean for you to carry the cross?

It might mean a small change in your life.

It might mean your life.

We have been carried. The time is now, for us to carry the cross to a world in love with kingdoms.

JEREMY, JUSTIN AND JORDAN WILLET are three brothers from Westminster, Maryland, who make up the rock band called Willet. The band partners with Food for the Hungry in making a difference in the lives of the poor around the world.

SPONSORSHIP BRINGS UNEXPECTED BLESSING

Last fall, one of Food for the Hungry's partnering musicians, WILLET, played at the Truth Exposed Festival in Winner, S.D. During their performance, band members took time to share with the audience about child sponsorship, encouraging people to sponsor a child through Food for the Hungry.

Lead vocalist Jeremy Willet asked for interested individuals to raise their hands, after which bass player Jordan Willet handed out child sponsorship packets to them. A man in the crowd stood up and began helping Jordan hand out packets. The man's wife raised her hand and asked for a girl. In response the man reached into the pile of packets, handed one to his wife and continued moving through the crowd.

Following the show, Jeremy Willet saw the same woman filling out the sponsorship forms. He walked over to her to thank her for sponsoring a child and to find out if she needed any help. As Jeremy approached, he noticed she was crying. "Jeremy," she said, "I need to tell you a story."

The woman went on to explain that years ago a doctor told her she would never have children. However this past year, she became pregnant. While still pregnant, she and her husband picked out the name, "Michelle" for their child. Unfortunately, she miscarried and lost the baby.

After listening to the appeal for child sponsorship, the woman decided that if she could not have a child of her own, the least she could do was help another child in need. She raised her hand and received a packet.

"She started crying again as she flipped over the packet of her new sponsored child," says Jeremy. Then the woman showed Jeremy the reason for her tears. Her child, a girl from Beho, Ethiopia, was named "Michelle."

Through their concerts, Willet speaks boldly about God's message of hope and transformation to thousands of music fans who are given the opportunity to sponsor a child and be God's instruments of change for families and communities in the hard places.

love.
+ blood.
+ forgiveness.
+ garments.
+ change.
- kingdoms.
+ salt.
+ water.=_____
The Kingdom of Jesus

Carry the cross with us. Help one orphaned child today for around $1/day.

www.carriedbook.com

epilogue.

For some time, we have heard people talk about how God is in the small things. We know this to be true and have seen it time and time again, but we feel compelled to remind people that God is in the big things too. He does big things and it's been our experience that when we share what He has done, we consistently see Him do more things right before our eyes.

In Acts Ch. 2, the Holy Spirit is poured out upon the early church at Pentecost. In one single day, more than 3,000 people put their faith and trust in Jesus Christ. That is big. So big, in fact, that it's the single-greatest-revival spoken of in the history of the world. We are not told in the Scriptures how the personal faith of those 3,000+ played out in the long run, but we sense that many of them were instrumental in the spreading of the Gospel to the known world.

Fast forward 2,000 years (give or take a decade or so). WILLET set out into 2009 with a goal of seeing 500 kids get sponsored. Before leaving for Africa in February, we were thankful for SIX. Four-hundred-ninety-four to go.

In the months that followed, God made a way for the stories to be told quite often, and before we knew it, the goal of 100 was reached. Four-hundred to go.

Fast forward to August 23, 2009.

WILLET just returned from Haiti, and Justin just returned from Mexico. There had been 375 sponsors acquired so far as we started another two-month run of The 500 Faces Tour. On this particular day, WILLET had the opportunity to lead worship and share the message at two large services in Silver Spring, MD. After the second service, 122 children were sponsored bringing our total for the year to 498!

For a band that plays 250 dates a year, sometimes the memories of shows seem to blend together, but this was a show I will not soon forget. As we took the stage, we were still two sponsors away from the goal. In the middle of the concert, we thanked the church for their huge response that morning, and told them that we were praying for the final two to come in. In the middle of our set, we had been singing "Hallelujah" and asking the crowd to join hands and sing along. From a long day of singing and preaching, my voice was starting to go out, but as I asked the crowd to grab the hands of those around them and sing "Hallelujah," our friend came running in the back doors holding up the final two envelopes showing that we had reached the goal of 500! As I told the crowd to give praise to God for the 500 sponsors the band built the music into a beautiful, loud chorus as the crowd began to sing on their own!

At the time of writing this book, we are still on the road and determined not to stop at 500! Both of us have committed our lives to helping the poor. WILLET is in the process of adopting our third village in Africa, this time in Mozambique, a place where 25,000 people share one clean-water well. It's time to bring hope to them now. In addition, we are launching a nationwide program called THE HUNGER STRIKE where we ask students to fast for 24-hours to raise money to sponsor children.[1] My (Jeremy) wife, Kathleen, has recently accepted the call to be a mom to eight orphaned children in Haiti as a full-time missionary where she will live amongst some of the poorest people in the world. I (Justin) know that God is calling our family to live and serve in another country full-time as well—we are just waiting patiently on Him to show us where. In the mean time, we know where our Jerusalem is (Taneytown), and our Judea (surrounding towns), our Samaria (Mexico) and the ends of the earth. We will not cease to go, take students, and meet Jesus wherever He is at work.

As we have traveled around the world and spent time with some of the most forgotten people, we have witnessed the diverse faces of poverty. Regardless of where you witness hopelessness, whether in the U.S. or in a third world country, several facts remain true:

---

[1] www.thehungerstrike.org

A hungry child is a child that needs food.

A child that is sick is a child in need of medicine.

A child sleeping on a sidewalk is a child that needs a bed.

A child that can't read is a child in need of education.

And most importantly, a child that is lost is a child that needs the Savior.

Jesus.

study guide.

Study Guide: Chapter 1

1. When was the last time that you felt uncomfortable in church? Explain.

2. How would you feel if God made you a promise, straight to your face and then 25 years went by before you ever saw it come true?

3. Who is your Lord and Savior?

Study Guide: Chapter 2

1. Jeremy used the words "God had other plans" several times through this chapter. Looking back through your life, are there times when you wanted to go a certain direction, but God had other plans?

2. When did you first learn about extreme poverty? What was your initial reaction? Has it changed?

3. Chapter 2 is titled *blood.* because the last sentence alludes to a series of events in Jeremy's life that ultimately changed the direction of the ministry of WILLET. Do you recall a turning point in your life where you said, "I can't go back to where I was?"

Study Guide: Chapter 3

1. Justin talked about the pain and hurt he experienced from his parent's divorce. Can you relate to this? If so, how do you deal with pain?

2. Do you harbor un-forgiveness in your heart toward someone? Pray now and ask God to help you make peace.

3. How is your relationship with Jesus Christ? Do you know Him more than the first day that you met Him?

4. Is God calling you into full time Christian service? If so, what does that look like? Youth Pastor? Missionary? Talk to your pastor or church leader about it, today!

Study Guide: Chapter 4

1. Some people pray to Jesus and claim to trust Him just so that they don't go to Hell some day. Why is this wrong?

2. Are you living in community with other Christians? Does this community look like the early church (Acts 2)?

3. Who is part of your spiritual garment? Why did you choose those people?

4. In Matthew 27:32, a man named Simon of Cyrene is compelled to help Jesus bear His cross. What do you make of this?

Study Guide: Chapter 5

1. We ask the question, "career or calling?" several times through this chapter. How would your life be different if your current career was replaced by your calling? If you don't have a career yet, where is your life headed? What are your goals, dreams, and steps to get there?

2. When you read about villages like Gorongosa in Mozambique, does it begin to bring perspective to your life? When hearing about 25,000 people sharing one clean-water well, does that bother you?

3. Chapter 5 ends with a journal entry from our trip to Africa in 2009. The theme of the entire article (later published in 6:8 Magazine, Fall 2009) is change. We have witnessed change in a small village in Africa. Has this story inspired

you to be a part of change within your community or another place in the world? If so, what kind of sacrifices will it require on your part?

Study Guide: Chapter 6

1. When you read the statistics about extreme poverty, what immediately runs through your mind? Write down your thoughts.

2. How have you noticed worship and social justice impacting today's culture? Do you recognize it as a way of life or simply a passing fad?

Study Guide: Chapter 7

1. Chapter 7 discusses the third (and final) group of kingdoms as "those who are so in love with the Kingdom of Jesus that they do nothing about it." Do you know anyone like this? Have you found yourself to be guilty of this way of living at some point in your life?

2. An in-depth look at salt is examined as not only being used for flavor, but also for preserving. One of the reasons that God destroyed Sodom and Gomorrah was because of a "neglect for the poor and needy." Do you feel God preserving your life to be among the poor and needy? John 12:8 reminds us that we "will always have the poor among you", whether you travel to a village in Africa, or across the street in your neighborhood. Where is God calling you?

Study Guide: Chapter 8

1. What does it mean for you to carry the cross?

2. There are so many injustices in the world. Which one does God want you to focus in on and make a difference therein?

3. What is a tangible way that you have seen someone carrying a cross lately?

4. You can probably come up with a thousand reasons why it is not feasible for you to sponsor a child today. Write down 1 reason why you could sponsor a child.

Scripture Study

1. Word study: *carried*

Deuteronomy 1:31	Luke 14:27
Isaiah 53:4, 63:9, 8:17,	Galatians 6:26
40:11, 46:4b	John 19:17
Leviticus 16:22	1 John 5:2

2. Word Study: *the poor*
Leviticus 19:9-10, 13-15
Deuteronomy 10:14-22, 15:7-11, 26:12
1 Samuel 2:8
Psalms 12:5, 112, 146:5-9
Proverbs 11:24-25, 14:31, 19:17, 31:8-9, 31:20
Isaiah 61:1-3
Jeremiah 22:15-17
Ezekiel 16:49
Amos 2:6-7
Micah 6:8
Malachi 3:5
Matthew 5:42, 25:31-36
Luke 3:10-14, 4:16-21, 6:17-26, 10:25-37, 12:33, 14:12-14
Acts 4:32-37, 10:4, 30-31
Romans 12:13
1 Corinthians 13:3, 2 Corinthians 8-9
Galatians 2:10
Ephesians 4:28
1 Timothy 5:3-10, 6:17-19
Hebrews 13:16
James. 2:1-18, 5:1-6
1 John 3:16-18

Additional Information: